TURNER'S TURN

TURNERS TURN

GERALDINE TURNER

TURNER'S TURN

A disarmingly honest memoir

First published in 2022 by New Holland Publishers
Sydney • Auckland

Level 1, 178 Fox Valley Road, Wahroonga, NSW 2076, Australia
5/39 Woodside Ave, Northcote, Auckland 0627, New Zealand

newhollandpublishers.com

A record of this book is held at the National Library of Australia.

ISBN 9781760794439

Group Managing Director: Fiona Schultz
Project Editor: Liz Hardy
Designer: Andrew Davies
Production Director: Arlene Gippert
Printed in Australia by SOS Print + Media Group

10 9 8 7 6 5 4 3 2 1

Keep up with New Holland Publishers:

 NewHollandPublishers

 @newhollandpublishers

Contents

For Brian
And the babies

Thank you to James Laurie
for encouraging me to write this book.

Foreword

When Geraldine was a teenager and already an accomplished performer, a journalist asked her what her future ambitions were. She said her ambition was for Australians to think of her as 'Our Geraldine' in the same way that people spoke of the great Gladys Moncrieff as 'Our Glad'. Looking back, she's now embarrassed at how brash that ambition seemed, and she believes that by no stretch of the imagination has she achieved that status. Well, maybe not, but if she has fallen short it's not by all that much.

Often we hear some performer's career described as stellar and wince because we know it's been something less than that, but in Geraldine's case that adjective has been more than earned. She has played with verve and panache just about all the great female roles in musical theatre and many memorable roles in straight theatre, captivating audiences since the seventies. We go to the theatre so we can be up close and personal to great stories being brought to life by great performances and when Geraldine was in a cast you knew you were going to get everything she could give. There was electricity in the theatre every time she entered stage left or stage right. Something special was about to happen. And it always did. I still remember her memorable performance as the witheringly honest Jenny in a wonderful revival of my own play *Don's Party*.

It's very hard to define what makes great actors so riveting. It's something to do with energy, presence, charisma and timing but finally for me it comes down to watchability. You simply can't take your eyes off them. There's a magic you can't understand but you love it. Geraldine has that in spades. She's delighted countless audiences with that magic for so long now that you assume that the confidence and panache you see on stage is what she is offstage. Not so, which is why her memoir is so surprising, touching and revealing. You might assume it's going to be simply a recollection of her many stage triumphs, which of course are there, but what's also there are the anxieties and insecurities and regrets that lie just under her confident surface.

Geraldine is still haunted by her past. An erratic, unpredictable and at times unbalanced mother whose love and approval she desperately sought but so seldom got. A father who was caring and loving when sober but violent and menacing when he was drunk. Brothers who never stopped fighting viciously and who at one Christmas gathering became so enraged that one threatened the others with a shotgun. One brother spent years in prison for manslaughter and Geraldine was the only family member compassionate enough to regularly visit him in prison. She still feels guilt and distress that she couldn't love her family more, but their behaviour makes the reasons more than understandable.

Geraldine is honest enough to admit that at times her own temper got the better of her and caused irreparable damage to some of her theatrical relationships, and how her hunger for the love and acceptance that never came from her mother caused her to tolerate far too much from male partners, but what emerges overall from this candid and very readable memoir is her warm heart, her anger at injustice, and her fragility. A casual insensitive remark from a random member of the public endured stoically in public can still cause her to weep buckets in private. It's still hard for her to understand the human cruelty she was exposed to in her family and still sees around her, because it's the very antithesis of her own forgiving nature. It's a great relief to finally read that this special person has at last found the partner she deserves and a life with him of relative contentment and peace.

This is the story of one of our all-time greatest stage performers and also the story of an admirable human being who overcame a nightmare upbringing to become very close to 'Our Geraldine'.

David Williamson
March, 2022

1

Time and Time Again

We're on the bus. I'm little. Perhaps it's my earliest memory. I'm not sure of anything, as this happens many times over my childhood years, not only on the bus, sometimes in department stores. She does it once at ballet. I scream and run down Charlotte Street in Brisbane, closely followed by my teacher. Some things blur over time. You learn to block things out. You want to. You need to. You learn to have a poker face to hide the hurt. A lot of it I don't remember. I have a good poker face my whole life. I can hide a lot of things.

My mother and I are on the bus.

Suddenly, Mum starts shouting, talking to someone who isn't there. She's swearing. She doesn't usually swear, unless she is having one of her 'fits' or is really cranky.

She rants. Then lies down in the aisle of the bus, starts pulling at her clothes and accusing the bus driver at the top of her voice.

'He wants to fuck me! Stop him! You want to fuck me, you friggin' bastard! Somebody do something!'

No-one on the bus does anything. They stare out the windows as if nothing is happening. I do too.

'She's not with me.'

I don't know the word 'embarrassed', but I feel it keenly. I want to disappear.

There is buzzing in my head.

Suddenly, she's sitting beside me again.

'What's up with you?' she says.

'Nothing.'

She slaps me. It hurts.

'You'd better not tell anyone! Don't tell your father.'

Years and years later, my father, four older brothers and I gather together the night before Mum's funeral and, after the boys pour accolades on me for managing to get meat and three veg on a plate for each of them, someone brings up 'the bus'.

'We didn't know you had it in you,' they say about the meal. None of my achievements has ever resulted in such praise from any of my family.

Turns out, Mum has done the bus routine with each of us and none of us has talked about it till now. We have all kept her secret.

Families ...

I was taken to a pantomime at the old Theatre Royal in Brisbane when I was five. I came home and apparently announced that I wanted to be on the stage. I don't remember this but my mother told me, over and over, as if to instil that memory. Perhaps I never said it. This was the beginning of my mother trying to live her life through me. It was always there, that pressure to please her. Nothing was ever enough. I was never enough.

She had wanted to be on the stage, but her father wouldn't allow it. She possessed a wonderful singing voice and I believe if she had really had the drive, she could have done it. Maybe I am being a little hard on her, saying that. In those days, a young woman was more likely to obey rather than rebel. She was born on 4 June 1913.

Mother, Grace Isabell Turner, nee Walker, did get a job, when she was a young girl, as a seamstress (she was a wonderful sewer and made all my clothes) and dresser for Bebe Scott, the half-sister of the great George Wallace, the wonderful Australian vaudeville star. Bebe was a well-known soubrette.

Mum was a fabulous raconteur. She spoke of dramas backstage, with Bebe and her boyfriend at the time, Mum having to cover the bruises from punch-ups before matinee days. I lapped up every story with relish. Mum, Issie as she was called, was a very funny woman. I used to love her stories, not only about backstage with Bebe, and there were countless tales of those, but the others about her early life.

She had a large family, sisters Florence, Nellie, and Pauline, brothers, Bill, Ernie and Mason. Mum was in the middle, Pauline was the youngest.

Mum always talked of how poor they were. Certainly, the war had brought on hard times. However, my grandfather, William, was a wool classer, and much admired, though he did like a drink. We would probably call him an alcoholic these days. His nickname was Ducky. He loved to go shooting, ducks in particular. Makes me feel ill to think of that, shooting and killing for sport. Ducky had a car in those early days, so really, how poor could they have been?

Mum had a knack for using drama for the best effects. She loved telling the story about going for a drive with the family when she was a small child, her sitting on a fruit box, with holes in her sweater. I have to question her version. Much more dramatic to be the forgotten child, not dressed properly … and without a proper seat! Still, I laughed every time she told of their driving along and her father suddenly saying, as he saw a car wheel rolling off into the bushes, 'Some poor sod has lost a wheel! That'll ruin their day.'

Suddenly, their car ground to a halt.

Mum shrieked, 'It was our wheel!!!' We laughed like drains every time.

She shared many stories, like the time she went to the local pool and asked a nice looking woman in the change room to mind her clothes. When she returned, the woman and Mum's things were gone. Mum had to walk all the way home in her bathing costume, with not even a towel to cover her up. She received glares from passers-by. It was certainly not the done thing for a young woman to be 'almost naked' in the street in those days.

Then there was the time she was at the vaudeville. She didn't have any extra money for sweets at interval. She noticed a well-dressed gentleman standing near the entrance. Mum stood next to him and pretended to cry. Real tears … such an actress!

'What's wrong, young lady?'

'I've lost my fare home.'

The nice gentleman handed her some coins and she went straight over, almost in front of him, silly her, and bought an ice cream. She felt hands on her shoulders, as he whipped her around to face him and shouted, 'I'm getting the police onto you!'

Mum used to relish telling how she slipped out of his clutches and ran off, with her ice cream intact.

'I was far too quick for him!' she would laugh as she recalled the incident.

She relayed all these stories as if she were a professional comedienne. I was enthralled every time. She also managed to include a new 'bit' each time to add to each story. I believe she did have talent. Her timing was excellent. You can't teach that.

My grandmother Helena died from an asthma attack, when Mum was very young. I never knew that until Auntie Nellie told me years later at my mother's funeral. I have asthma too. I don't really know anything about Helena. She was gone from the family's lives so soon that there were no funny stories, no memories really, of her existence.

So, as happened a lot back then, the eldest daughter, Florrie, stayed home, gave up any thought of a life of her own and virtually brought up the children. She died at twenty-eight from kidney disease, having had no life to speak of. My cousin, Carol, Aunty Pauline's daughter, told me poor Florrie lost her sight towards the end of her life.

Growing up, we lived at 51 Wedd Street, Spring Hill, Brisbane, an inner-city working-class suburb, which is quite 'chi chi' now. The cottage is still there, dwarfed by high rises. When I go to Brisbane, I always find time to go there, sit out the front of the house in a car. Invariably, I burst into tears. I feel a sense of loss for those early years in Spring Hill; while lots of those memories are not good at all, your mind tends to play tricks on you, as you get older. The yearning for the old days comes from a happy place. Reality is pushed to the back of your mind. The bad memories are buried deeply within you as you try to search for meaning, a reason for it all.

After the panto and my alleged declaration of stage ambitions, I was sent to ballet class at age five, to Desley Horton's suburban dance studio. It was a trek to the suburbs for dance class. More bus horrors.

My mother had it in her mind that I would become a great ballerina. 'Everything's lovely. It's so glamorous! You get a huge bouquet at the end of the performance. You choose one rose and give it to your dance partner. Everyone wants to be you.'

This was her fantasy, not mine. Mum loved that all the costumes are pretty and everything looks so clean up on the stage at the ballet. She banged on about cleanliness her whole life. She thought sex was dirty. She loved everything nice and clean and well scrubbed. With her ongoing strange behaviour, it is not a stretch to imagine that Mum might well have been abused sexually as a child.

So, I was to be her little ballerina. I was not allowed to play any more. I had to practise. I remained with Miss Horton for a few years, before going to the great Phil Danaher, where my dance skills blossomed. At Miss Horton's, I was in a ballet group called 'The Little Five'. We soon appeared on television on a children's show called *Cottee's Happy Hour*. By then we were the Channel 7 Junior Ballet ... my first job in show business at seven.

One day I recall some children visiting next door and Mum, for some inexplicable reason, allowing me to play with them. This was unheard of. She certainly never let me play again after this day.

For weeks she had been making huge butterfly wings, sewing, gluing, painting, for a duo I was to do on television with a girl from dance class, Margaret Ross. Up until then, I had only appeared in 'group' numbers. So, Mother saw this as a big opportunity to shine. Her little ballerina was in the making. Of course, as fate would have it, the one time I was allowed to play, I broke my left elbow, and I am left-handed, so it turned out to be a big problem for me for a number of weeks. Dad was getting ready to take me to the hospital. I was crying in pain, with my bone having been displaced. Mother, on the other hand, was shouting at me, 'You'd better not come back with plaster on that arm, my girl! You won't be able to do the butterfly dance!'

I was in a cast for six weeks. Mum made me sit and watch Margaret Ross do a solo version of the butterfly dance the next week. She was furious.

'That should've been you up there! That is the end of games for you, my girl.'

In 2018, while doing a concert in Brisbane, I received a note from Margaret Ross, who was in the audience. She came backstage and it was great to see her after all those years. She remembered the incident well as her one claim to fame! We laughed. It was lovely to see her again and to come full circle.

Mum did take me to see wonderful ballets. There were some good times. She took me to see Margot Fonteyn and we waited at stage door, with autograph book in hand, for what seemed like hours. When Miss Fonteyn eventually emerged, looking and smelling divine, I was too shy to ask for her autograph. Miss Fonteyn brushed past me and the scent of that perfume filled the air. You know, I have searched for years for that perfume to no avail. All these years later, I just have to close my eyes and I can smell it as if it happened yesterday.

I haven't spoken about my father. Leo Noel Turner was an only child, born in 1914. His family was from Dalby in Queensland. He was brought up Catholic, but changed to Anglican when he married my mother. Dad was a kind, though weak man. When he drank he became violent. My brothers always said that Mum egged him on. I disagree. There is never an excuse for hitting a woman.

I remember arguments, like when Dad picked up one end of the tablecloth of a perfectly set dinner table and pulled it out aggressively, so that plates, food, cups went flying, smashing into pieces, hitting the walls, tomato sauce everywhere, everything in total disarray. He then said to Mum in a rough, loud voice, 'Now, clean it up!'

The vision of Mum crying, on her hands and knees, trying to clean the total mess, has never left me.

He never hit me. Before I was born, if one of the boys was naughty, he would line them up and belt them all for good measure. By the time I came along that had ceased. However, many a time we would be at Emergency getting stitches in Mum's head or some such.

And yet, Dad loved his family and wanted us all to get along. We didn't, especially the boys. There were many holes in the walls from missed punches from my brothers' fights. Such a lot of violence and alcohol! Dad drank a lot. So did Ralph and Noel. They weren't happy drunks. I have observed this over the years with a few friends. Everything is going along pleasantly, until that person has one more drink, and everything changes and that person becomes Mr Hyde.

It is easy to toss it off and blame 'the drink'. But are these people, in this case my father and two older brothers, being their true selves when sober, and alcohol switches something in the brain, or is the violent, loaded-up-with-alcohol person the real true self? I don't know.

Alcohol played a large part in my family dynamic. Mum didn't drink, except on special occasions, when she would have a shandy. I have never been a big drinker. I saw what it could do. In fact, every time the family got together there was a fight of some kind. There is one surviving photo of our whole family at my brother Ray's wedding. I was a teenager and the bridesmaid. That snap was taken just before an embarrassing punch-up between Ralph and Noel at Lennons Hotel in Brisbane. None of the boys liked Noel. I don't know why.

I hated Christmas. I dreaded it. It meant much drinking, followed by an argument and physical violence. Every year. To this day, I really don't like that time of year … all the family movies that are shown, the advertisements about happy families. It is all too much when you have never had those close family moments and you feel inadequate. I wished I had been born into another family. Sometimes I pretended I was. I made up stories and dance routines and the notion of an altogether different life. 'Maybe I was adopted. I am not like any of them.'

There were no baby photos of me. It was only when I grew up I realised that we were poor. That was the reason for the lack of photos. They probably didn't own a camera.

I know we didn't have a phone until I was a teenager. When television came to Queensland, we rented a set you had to put coins in to make it work. We had it for years. Often you'd be in the middle of a favourite show when the TV would go clunk and switch off, as there were no more coins left. We missed the end of many a good show.

Dad was a truck driver, so he was away a lot. Mum had to manage the finances, something she did not do well. She bought fabric all the time to make dresses for me. She spent money wildly on things we could hardly afford. I have inherited that quality from her. I have never been good with money, unfortunately. However, I am generous with money, as my mother was. I cannot bear meanness or miserable people. Life is too short. It was Mike Todd, one of Elizabeth Taylor's husbands who said, 'I have been broke many times in my life, but I have never been poor. Being poor is a state of mind.'

Dad was always away working. In the school holidays, Dad would take me in his truck sometimes and we'd stay overnight in a motel. Mum would pack sandwiches for us. I had my own lunch box. I loved sitting up there in the cabin and spending some time with my father. I did love him. I was his only little girl. When he was sober, he was a very gentle man. I was scared of Mr Hyde. What made him drink and become violent with Mum? Why did he turn after a few drinks? Was it something that was genetic and therefore passed on to my brothers? Whatever, it really was like living with two entirely different fathers.

Sometimes, when Dad had a bit to drink, not too much, he used to say our real name was Dunne, not Turner. Mum would stand behind him and mouth, 'Don't take any notice. He's drunk.'

We knew Grannie, Dad's mother, who lived down the road with Maggie, Dad's cousin, in a tiny, dark cottage that looked like it was part of a frightening fairytale. All of my other grandparents had died before my birth. We visited Grannie often, until she died when I was quite young. Maggie died soon after.

Many years later when Dad died, two years after Mum, we received his death certificate and it said Dad's name was Leo Dunne. After looking at Mum and Dad's wedding certificate at the same time, it stated that his mother, Kathleen, was deceased at the time of their wedding. So who was Grannie? Was Dad adopted or merely taken care of by this woman we called Grannie? Did the Dunnes, being a rural, Catholic family, disown Kathleen after she became pregnant and then she travelled to Brisbane? Dad's father, Grannie's husband, had a fruit barrow and was arrested after a fight one day and dumped in a cell overnight, where he died from his injuries. All of this happened before I was born.

After a little research, I have found out that Kathleen, dad's birth mother, had a daughter before Dad but she died at two months of age. She also had a daughter three years after she had Dad. That girl died at age two. No father's names appear on any of Kathleen's children's birth certificates. At what time then did Grannie start taking care of Dad? Dad clearly remembered his birth mother because Dad used to sing to me when I was a baby. He'd sing, 'I'll Take You Home Again, Kathleen' and he used to say it was his mother Kathleen's favourite song. As he began the song, apparently my bottom lip would tremble and I would begin to weep. Obviously, my appreciation of the emotion and the power of music was present at an early age. Maybe it was Dad's singing voice that moved me as a baby. He had been part of a barbershop quartet in his youth and he did play the harmonica very well. Whatever it was, this baby girl had a great appreciation of what music can do for the soul.

Clearly, the Turners had either formally or informally adopted my father. His birth and death certificates say his name was Leo Neal Dunne, but he was Leo Noel Turner at the time he married my mother in 1936.

All of this remains a mystery. I'm sure someone knew, but they are all gone now. I may still have family in Dalby. Those never-spoken-of family secrets are really fascinating.

I think my mother loved my father, although it was hardly a happy marriage. One of her brothers, I think Uncle Mason, brought him to their house. She used to speak of the first time she saw Dad walking down the street in a sailor's outfit (goodness knows why as he was not in the armed forces) and she spoke of his bell-bottom trousers swinging as he walked, obviously a very exciting memory for her.

They married at All Saints Anglican Church at Wickham Terrace in Brisbane. Mum often talked of her shame about Catholic nuns turning up at the house when she was pregnant with Ralph, my eldest brother, accusing her of living in sin, as she was not married in the Catholic Church. If you do the addition, Ralph was born about seven months after their wedding, an absolute 'no-no' in those times.

My brothers' names were Ralph Gordon, Noel William, Raymond Mason, and Leigh Geoffrey. Really, my parents had two families. The three older boys were born two years apart. Then six years passed. Then Leigh was born and four years later, I came along. So, Leigh and I grew up together, as if we were the only two children in the family.

Mum said she hid away for most of her pregnancy with me, because women of that age shouldn't be having babies, code for shouldn't be having sex. She was thirty-seven. In fact, as I have suggested, Mum was uneasy about anything to do with sex. We were never allowed to have our bedroom doors closed for instance. We'd be up to no good.

Mum said to me once, many years later, 'Those orgasm things. I never had one of those.' It was such a sad statement. She had blurted it out.

I think that conversation took place around the same time Mum was taking a course in ikebana, the Japanese art of flower arranging, so she thought she had her finger on the pulse of what it was to be a modern woman. Hence her sharing of that fact! I wish I had had the foresight to question her a little more. I regret it. This was the only time my mother had ever been so open with me about anything sexual.

I believe with all my being that Mum must have been abused. How else can I explain the bus horrors? And why did being on the bus trigger this memory? Something really bad had happened to her and it informed the rest of her life.

I was one of those girls who thought I was dying when I got my first period. I hid in my room after hiding my underwear. Later, I heard Mum shouting, 'Geraldine! Come here!' Naturally, I was scared.

I knew she must have found the underwear. I started to cry. She shoved a book into my hands and told me to read it. That was that.

Mum went to the doctor, Doctor Marks, only once before I was born, and he told her, 'I think we are storing up a little bundle for heaven.'

What a thing to say! Mum thought I would be stillborn. How wrong was that doctor. I popped out, very much alive, and with the biggest brown eyes. My brother Noel, twelve at the time, apparently said, 'Get the bewdy lights on her!'

I can only imagine the joy of having a girl at last, after four boys, but the suffocation that was to follow and the inability to please my mother has coloured my life. I was named Geraldine Gail (Mum wanted to spell it

Gale, as I was born in a storm, but they got the spelling wrong on the birth certificate) and it was on 23 June 1950.

My early childhood was filled with ballet class and practice. I must have been taken by my mother to see musical films, as I often used to walk down the street, breaking into song and my own choreography, wondering why the passers-by didn't know the choreography somehow, like they did in the movies, and join in. It made me a little cross that they hadn't bothered to step up, take responsibility and learn it.

At home, apart from the regular domestic violence, which made me go very quiet and try to disappear, and the continuing odd behaviour of my mother, I loved ironing day. Mum would sit me on the ironing table and we'd play a game. I would say a word, and she would sing a song with that word in the first line. She knew more songs than anyone I have ever known. She possessed a lovely, quite naturally open singing voice, with a soprano range and a great belt. She understood phrasing as well.

I had two toys, a teddy bear, which I still have, and a beautiful doll named Rosemary, which had long blonde plaits. Oh I loved her. I think Leigh and I had a skirmish one day and Rosemary was damaged. Mum took her to the doll hospital and I never saw her again. I kept asking, then gave up and quietly resented Mum for it. I realised only when I grew up that Mum probably couldn't afford to have the doll fixed.

She lied to me about the dentist as well. She said he was going to put some ointment in my mouth to stop my toothache. I woke up, having had gas and eight teeth removed, bending over a basin, coughing up blood. Maybe she was attempting to protect me, but it sure didn't feel like that.

They're skewed sometimes, the things you think as a child. Every Christmas, Dad's work (he worked for Cobb & Co) had a big party. Santa came and each of the children of the workers was called up to receive a gift from Santa. I used to see fabulous presents – bikes (I was never allowed to have a bike. I might fall off and not be able to dance) dolls, doll's houses – given to other children, while I would receive a tiny offering like crayons and a colouring book. I wondered for all those years why Santa didn't like me very much. I was good, wasn't I? I tried to be better each year, but it didn't make any difference. I still received insignificant gifts from Santa. Of course, it depended on the amount of money the parents contributed each year, but how was I to know that? It's a bit rough growing up thinking Santa doesn't like you. I imagined I was on the naughty list and had no idea why.

Not long after I met my husband, Brian, who is a kind soul at heart, I told him about losing Rosemary, my beloved doll and how it had affected me. The next time he came back from a trip to Melbourne, he had bought me a beautiful blonde-haired doll from a wonderful doll shop that used to be in the Block Arcade. He had told the shop assistant the story and emphasised that he knew it couldn't ever replace Rosemary, but that he felt the need to do something. So, darling Millie lives in my study to this day. She sits on the piano, looking quite happy to be there. She has blonde hair and a lovely, expressive face, just like my Rosemary. She sits next to my teddy. Brian's mother made a lovely checked jacket and bow tie for him to freshen him up. He likes it.

Throughout my very early years, my mother had a friend called Norie Coghlan. I have no idea how they met. It was a strange friendship by today's standards as they never went out together, or met for afternoon tea, or to go shopping. Norie used to come to our house when we lived at Spring Hill, each day after work at around six o'clock. She often sat in the bathroom as I took my bath, talking to Mum, but mostly, they would sit at the kitchen table and have a cup of tea and talk of everyday things. Norie was a secretary, who had lost her fiancé to a car accident. Actually, he had been run over and killed. Mum told us that he was a married man and that Norie could never have married him. That was never talked about. None of us ever let on to Norie that we knew that Frank, her fiancé, was married.

Norie lived in a rather grand house up on Gregory Terrace, with her sister, Bridie. Norie was a tiny, feisty Irish woman. The reason I mention her at all is to speak of my mother's kindness. When we moved to Annerley, those daily visits ceased. I guess they kept in touch over the years, and saw each other sometimes, perhaps going to a matinee of a show together, because when I was in my final year of school, studying for my final exams, Norie moved in with us. I don't know what had happened to Bridie by then, but it was made known to my mother and father that Norie had dementia and had no-one to take care of her. They immediately took her in. She lived with us for about a year, with Mum fussing over her and being genuinely kind to her, kinder than I had ever seen her be to anyone.

Norie often disappeared and Mum would search the streets endlessly in Dutton Park, where we first rented after we lost our house in Annerley. Mum always found Norie, brought her home and bathed her, while Norie mumbled irrationally about her Frank, as if he were still alive.

It was distracting for me during my final school exams, to have Norie hanging about outside my bedroom, talking constantly to herself. It was disconcerting as she could be discovered lurking outside your room, or wandering up and down the hallway in the middle of the night. We got through it all until one day, not long after my exams, Norie took a turn, a stroke, and she was carted away in an ambulance. She died not long after. It was a sad end.

As Dad would have done, Mum would give a person the last coins in her purse, or indeed stretch a meal to include anyone in need. It was an extremely good quality to possess, one that I am happy to have inherited. They both possessed an innate social conscience.

Meanwhile, at ballet, I auditioned for my first big professional job, *Aladdin*, produced by Tibor Rudas, who was the producer of the Three Tenors many years later.

It was a matinee show performed each day. Hazel Phillips, Australian actress and TV personality, was Aladdin. Each night, a variety show called *Oriental Cavalcade* played. Will Mahoney, American comedian and the great musical star Evie Hayes's husband, was in the show, as were sight acts like Joe Ballangue, whose act was playing the mouth organ with his nose while smoking a cigarette or eating a banana. I was entranced. To this day, I love sight acts. I still have his autograph, which includes his signature and a hand-drawn harmonica.

Everything about being a part of the show was so exciting, especially the time I was chosen to be in my costume at night, before *Oriental Cavalcade*, as a cigarette girl, carrying a tray full of cigarettes in the foyer, to hand out free to the 'ladies'. I was eight years old. Wouldn't pass the pub test these days!

My very first line on the professional stage was to a character called 'So Shy'. It was the intro to a number of hers: 'Please sing for us, So Shy.'

I remember the smell of greasepaint, as you entered the stage door of Her Majesty's Theatre in Brisbane, and the rickety stairs up to the dressing rooms. That was the beginning of my love affair with theatres and empty stages. Even today, I am always the first to arrive at the theatre for a performance. I always have been very early, to everything, but especially to work. I love to walk out onto the empty stage before a performance and just … be. Before anyone arrives, apart from stage crew, I imagine all those who came before me. It is a way to honour the past and all the ghosts who spur me on to do my best each night.

Of course I also remember lining up each Thursday for our pay packets. I bought a gold watch from my earnings.

When my brother Leigh was thirteen, and I was nine, he was allowed to catch the bus to town with a friend to go to the pictures in the holidays. I must have performed 'something shocking' this day for Mum to tell Leigh he had to take me. He was given enough money for the movie tickets and the bus fare and an ice cream each. After the movie, I had dropped something, so crawled under my seat to look for it. When I got up I couldn't see Leigh or his friend. I walked to the foyer. They were nowhere. So I decided to walk home. I remember clearly that I was not scared. I had a great sense of direction. Even now, I can revisit a city and find a restaurant or shop I visited years before.

I knew which way the bus went, as I had stared out the window for years on end with Mother and her dramas on the bus. So I walked and walked. It was a few miles. It was dark by the time I arrived home. I could hear Mum and Dad shouting at and belting poor Leigh, who was wailing.

'Where is she? Where is she?'

'I don't know.' Leigh was awash with tears.

'I'm home. It's okay,' I piped up.

I don't remember any relief or hugs. I never remembered hugs. Mum didn't touch us much. I know that Leigh was not forgiven for some time and it was certainly the end of trips to town without Mum.

Sometimes, Mum would take me to The Shingle Inn in Edward Street after ballet class. That was sheer bliss. I loved it there, the waitresses with perky caps and uniforms, with crisp, frilly aprons, and the sign, which read, 'We use real butter in all our cakes'.

It was always a treat to visit. The owners had a similar restaurant called, Haddon Hall in George Street, but it wasn't as exciting as The Shingle Inn. Mum would treat me to a fairy cake, or a scone with jam and cream, or a sponge. The restaurant had booths and lovely wooden panelling. You always noticed older women, alone, ordering the roast of the day. This was a time when a single woman would not usually eat in a restaurant alone, wouldn't ever consider it. But The Shingle Inn spelt safety for a single woman, and the weekly opportunity to have a roast dinner. No person who lived alone would ever bother to cook an entire roast for herself.

The Shingle Inn has gone now, but on a recent visit to Brisbane, in November 2020, to appear in the Lord Mayor's Gala Concert, I arrived at rehearsal and noticed a sign at the Town Hall. It seems The Shingle Inn is being reconstructed within the Town Hall, using the original wood panelling. It won't be the same, but I look forward to going there in the future. I do hope they make the same cakes. Their passionfruit sponge was always a winner for me. I am longing to see the old sign, 'We use real butter in all our cakes'.

2

Now I See

I move to Miss Danaher's Dance School around the time the family move to Annerley, across the river. A new build, rather humble, with a mortgage that Mum doesn't pay regularly and we end up losing the house a few years later and rent for the rest of my parents' lives. Mum is too busy buying things (she has great taste), making new clothes for me, buying things on the 'never never' from travelling salesmen, to ever worry about trifling matters such as paying our mortgage. I am at Danaher's ballet school from age nine to seventeen and make lifelong friends.

Throughout those early years and into my teens, we visited my many cousins most weekends when we could. Carol (Caz), Jill and Susan, Lynne, Coralie and Wendy were always supportive and great friends. My cousin, Carol, who is Auntie Pauline's daughter and a Gold Coast resident, is like the sister I never had. I love her. There were great times together, girl secrets and many laughs always. We remain close. In fact, Carol's son, Sandro Colarelli, is a very well-known Brisbane actor. I have worked with him, happily on a few occasions.

When Sandro was little, he and his brother and sister, who used to call my mother Auntie Grandma, had a family dog. It was Caz's Maltese terrier, named Omar, after Omar Sharif. One day Mum and Dad were visiting and they all went to the beach. Mum was quite heavy at that time and plonked down onto the beach hard, inadvertently sitting on Omar. They rushed him to the vet but there was nothing they could do. Caz and her husband Tony told the kids he was at the hospital while they desperately tried to get another dog who looked like Omar. They did and a few days later brought the new Omar home, where he lived a long life. Mum never got over it. Sandro told me they all knew it wasn't Omar, but they shut up and went along with it to please their parents and not to make Auntie Grandma feel even worse.

This was the dog that Caz used to say called her Carol. Mad. I heard him once. It was a kind of howl crossed with a yelp. It did sound a bit like he was saying Carol. He was named after a great actor, after all. Omar had good diction for a dog.

Auntie Pauline, Carol's mother, was also weird about sex. Something had certainly happened to those girls in that family. Auntie Pauline, like Mum, was obsessed with cleanliness, and obsessed with Carol 'doing the right thing, not being up to no good', just like Mum. Auntie Pauline was hard on Caz, when she started going out with boys. Those were the days when, if you were lucky, you would just manage a peck goodnight with a boy. Nevertheless, Auntie Pauline would make Caz remove her underwear to be inspected.

At least Mum didn't do that. I'm sure if she had thought of it, she might have.

Jill Walker, one of my other cousins, has a great singing voice as well. She enjoyed a career in Queensland, singing with bands. Those Walker cousins, the daughters of Mum's brothers, did not grow up with the same 'madness' that Caz and I had to navigate growing up with our mothers, as they had mothers who were not those crazy Walker girls.

I must, at this point, mention a primary schoolteacher who was a great influence on me. Miss Sheila Buggy cast me in the leading role in primary school in *Soot and the Fairies*, a cantata, opposite my classmate, John Meehan, who of course went on to become a world famous ballet dancer. Years later, John was in the audience at my cabaret debut in New York, along with

Roslyn Anderson, a famous dancer herself. She had been at Danaher's with me, before going on to the Australian Ballet and Netherlands Dance Theatre and a sensational career.

Miss Buggy inspired me. I was to work much later down the track with Miss Buggy's brother, Brian Buggy, who was the conductor of *No, No, Nanette*.

At the same time, my mother was taking me to more shows like *The Merry Widow*, with June Bronhill. I adored the theatre. June, in that show, is one of my earliest memories of a star performance.

I loved films too. When the film of *West Side Story* opened in Brisbane when I was in my early teens, it played for ten weeks. I went every week, ten times. I think, apart from loving the dancing, the score, the story, the drama, I kept going each week, hoping there would be a different, happy ending this time. Also, I was in love with all those wonderful dancing boys.

I did dance class three times a week, passing my RAD exams up to Intermediate. We also rehearsed Sundays for upcoming shows. As well as end-of-year concerts, we performed in *Christmas in Storyland* each year at the Town Hall. By then, the performing arm of the studio was called Ballet Theatre of Queensland. I performed in *The Nutcracker* and *Swan Lake* Act II, *Les Sylphides*, as well as other original ballets. I was in the corps, much to my mother's chagrin, apart from playing Franz in *The Nutcracker* while I was young enough.

Around ten years of age, I did my next professional season, for Borovansky Ballet, which later evolved into the Australian Ballet. I was a rat in *The Sleeping Princess*, which starred the great Kathleen Gorham. We played Her Majesty's Theatre in Brisbane for a number of weeks. I loved it. Even as a child, I remember loving the discipline of performing. I still have my autograph book from those days. The young woman who was in charge of us children, a dancer herself in the company, wrote in all of our autograph books when the season ended. We shared what she had written amongst us. I read things in some of the other girls' books like, 'You'll go far with your talent' or 'What a great little performer you are'.

In my book she wrote, 'A lovely little girl with a pretty smile. Stay as sweet as you are and keep on smiling'.

Even at my young age, I realised that this was code for 'You have no talent and I don't know what else to say'.

Meanwhile, during these years at ballet theatre, Ken McCaffrey, one of the dancers, started a breakaway group called Queensland Revue Theatre. We performed revues and 'potted' musicals. For instance, we did *The Pajama Game* and I played Mabel (I was a tad young for it, I know). Then I played Kim in *Bye Bye Birdie*, a show I love, as it was the first J. C. Williamson musical I ever saw with my mother. From that moment, I yearned to have a life in musicals.

Meanwhile, in my early teens, it was decided without my input, to send me to a private girls' school, St Margaret's Anglican Girls' School. My father couldn't afford it so my eldest brother, Ralph, whom I did not know really as he left home soon after I was born, decided to pay for my private schooling. I loved school. I have friends to this day from school. However, I always felt like the poor kid, as ski trips and extras were not a part of my life there. My brother Ralph later married and had two sons. Years later, I found out that he believed I had wasted my education by becoming an actress. He never talked of me with his children. If ever I was on television, he made them switch the channel. It is hurtful still to think of that.

While at school, I won the Dickens Fellowship Reading Competition each year for the school. My House, Tennyson, won the Shakespeare play competition each year (acted and/or directed by me) and of course I performed in the Gilbert and Sullivan productions, playing Captain Corcoran in *HMS Pinafore* and Nanki-Poo in *The Mikado* (I was tall and I could sing those boy roles).

I cried on the last day of school. It seemed to me the world opening up and allowing the freedom of making decisions for myself was scary, nothing to rebel against. I have always preferred having rules and pushing against them. I have spent my life doing that.

Two incidents still make my stomach go weak. We had two regular principals and an Anglican nun, Sister Jean Marie, as the third principal of the school. The sub-senior school dance was coming up and we could ask a boy. We could wear lipstick but no other makeup, and we were not allowed fancy hairdos. Sister Jean Marie had already relished pouring a bucket of cold water over one of the boarder's heads as she had been to the hairdresser. Of course her hair had been ruined. We were to introduce our partner to the line of teachers in the hall and to Sister Jean Marie. Of course, I rebelled and wore mascara. I didn't introduce my date, Paul Charlton, as I knew they'd notice my eye makeup.

In the middle of a dance on the dance floor, I suddenly felt hands on my shoulders from behind. I was swung around. It was Sister Jean Marie, who shouted, 'Go and wash your face immediately!!!' The music stopped. Everyone stared.

Humiliated, I fled to the trough outside and removed my eye makeup amidst floods of tears. Paul and my friends came running out to me.

Suddenly that girl with chutzpah appeared. I am always at my best when my back is against the wall. Instead of leaving and letting Sister win, I marched straight back into the hall with Paul on my arm, a smile on my face (ever the actress) and proceeded to go along the line, introducing him to all the teachers. When I got to Sister Jean Marie, she said, 'Are you enjoying the dance, dear?'

'Very much, thank you, Sister!'

The following year, I asked a very posh rich boy to take me to the dance. I remember he picked me up in a flash car, but really, he was as boring as bat shit! We lived in a most ordinary, rather boring 1950s new build in Annerley. Still, I asked my father if he could be 'discovered' in the lounge room as my date arrived, in a jacket (thank God he owned one) and smoking a pipe. Obviously I thought that was sophisticated, that it would disguise our suburban existence and that a pipe-smoking, jacketed father would show my date that we lived in a mansion.

Dad did it! Got to love him for that!

That second incident at school is emblazoned across my brain. The first day back after the Christmas holidays, was the day prefects and house captains were always announced to the whole school at assembly. I had been the captain of the school debating team for a number of years and we had much success. However, I withdrew from the team towards the end of my sub senior year to appear in one of the revues at Queensland Revue Theatre.

I half expected, hoped, that I would be named prefect and a house captain of Tennyson, as I had done my share of things for the school, had won many prizes, and I think I possessed some leadership qualities. It was apparent, as Sister Jean Marie read out the names, that my name was not there. Each house had two captains that year … all but Tennyson, which had one. I can only surmise that my name had been erased.

Even so, I sat there and sucked it up. No matter, I thought.

At assembly's end, Sister dismissed everyone but asked the senior school to remain and move to the front of the hall. She then said, 'I am now going to tell you all why Geraldine Turner was not made a prefect or house captain.'

Embarrassingly, right then and there, I began what I call 'humping crying' … you know, loud, uncontrollable sobbing, with body convulsing and strange, almost prehistoric sounding grunts exploding from a secret, deep place within. So not cool. As she went on, 'She wore makeup to the school dance and she withdrew from the debating team to do … a revue!'

The way she said 'revue', rolling that 'R' was as if I were a teenage girl working in a sleazy strip club. It was so humiliating, cruel and uncalled for.

Just a few years ago, I was invited back to school to be the guest at an arts festival in my honour. It's a wonder I agreed, but many years had passed. I had changed and I wanted to go back. I am thought of and spoken of at that school these days as a true achiever and someone the girls should aspire to be like; an old girl of significance. My keynote speech to the girls at assembly was about 'being enough'.

The postscript to this story is that in 1974, when I was playing Petra in *A Little Night Music* at Her Majesty's Theatre in Melbourne, I received a note one day from Jean Muir (formerly Sister Jean Marie). I had heard she had left the Order. She said in the note that she had followed my career with pride; that she was in the audience and would love to come backstage to see me after. I felt my stomach go weak and fall.

As she approached me after the show, I said, awkwardly, that I didn't know what to call her. She said, 'Call me Jean, dear.'

I couldn't. Didn't call her anything. And what was this calling me 'dear'? After congratulations on the performance and some awkward small talk, I summed up the courage.

'You never liked me at school, did you?'

She paused. Then said, 'Let's face it, dear. You were never a school girl.'

I graduated high school in 1967 at seventeen. I wanted to perform, but Dad made me go to teachers' college to have something to fall back on. Those two years at college turned out to be the happiest two years. I made more lifelong friends, Maxine, Kathy and Pam, and I would share the petrol costs of Maxine's FJ Holden, as she ferried us to and from college. I think I laughed more in that car than I had ever laughed in my life. We remain firm friends to this day.

I announced to Mum I was giving up ballet school to pursue my singing. She was furious, but came round when I won the very first *New Faces* competition on television, when I was just seventeen. Mother realised I could really sing. She enrolled me with a teacher at Queensland Conservatorium, when she realised she could have a budding singing star on her hands, rather than a ballerina.

'You must learn properly. You must take singing seriously. You must practise and develop your voice in the correct way. And you must always wear expensive shoes. One good pair is worth more than several pairs of cheap ones. People will know you have class.'

She was right about sending me to the Conservatorium. And you know what? I have always loved great shoes.

During *New Faces*, I sang 'The Sweetheart Tree' in the heats, 'Alfie' in the semi, where I received a perfect score from Bernard King, TV personality judge, and 'Something Wonderful' in the final. One of the judges, Joan Whalley, who ran Twelfth Night Theatre in Brisbane for a number of years, bought me a gown to wear in the final. I am so touched by her generosity to this day. Mum had made me a long, maroon velvet coatdress for the semifinals. It puckered everywhere. Velvet can be unforgiving to work with. I had argued with Mum about the outfit. Still, a perfect score for my song was a great result. I think the fact that my costume had looked less than perfect led Ms Whalley to take me out to buy a gown for the following week's final. Some may have seen it as favouritism. Perhaps it was. But I was grateful.

Just after the final competition, some of the contestants, including me, appeared in a concert. I had agreed to sing at the wedding of one of the male contestants in a few weeks time. Naturally, after this concert, I felt safe enough to accept a lift home from him and one of his friends. When I noticed we were not going in the right direction, I asked what was going on. He told me not to worry. They had to pick up something from his friend's house. It wouldn't take long.

We arrived at the house. It was a long drive to somewhere on the outskirts of Brisbane, somewhere almost rural. They grabbed at me and took me inside the house. The men told me to lie on the bed. I knew what was about to happen. I pleaded with them to take me home to no avail. I was frightened. I froze. I shut down completely. It was as if I were outside my body looking in. I became very quiet and put on my poker face. There were two of them and they were big guys. Instinctively, I knew not to fight, but later, it was difficult for me not to blame myself. I must have let it happen. I had no bruises, after all. I should have fought to get out of the house. How could I have stopped this? Could I have done something more? I was feeling all those things that all young women in this situation feel. Ashamed.

Only one of them took part. The other watched. When it was over, I asked again, tearfully, for them to take me home. I had no idea where we were.

They took me home. Dropped me off. I told no-one, ever. This is the first time I have spoken of it.

I said to my mother a few days later, 'I don't want to sing at that wedding anymore.'

Mum said, 'But you have agreed. Don't be ridiculous. You must do it.'

I couldn't see a way out, other than telling Mum everything. I know she'd have blamed me. I couldn't.

So two weeks later, I sang at my rapist's wedding.

Now, looking back on the incident, which I had all but blocked out for years as a way of coping, I know I was a smart young girl to behave in the way I did. It could have escalated quickly into a more violent situation if I hadn't. At the time, I thought I was a wimp. I thought the fault was mine. I thought I couldn't tell anyone because they wouldn't believe me, especially my mother.

As the years have gone by, I have learned that rape is not about sex. It is about power and control. I had won the competition and he needed to prove something, to get the better of me.

It is extraordinary that all these years later, women are still blamed.

Women are still scared to speak up. Women are still maligned in court. Women's reputations are still destroyed. Not much has changed.

I was just seventeen. It certainly took the shine off my win. I chose to push on and put this horrific episode to the back of my mind, as best I could. I find, as I write, that I am still embarrassed by it and realise I have not fully let go of my 'I must have done something to allow this to happen' scenario. Sexual assault is not something you get over. Rather, you adjust somehow and learn to absorb it until it becomes a part of the person you are, as you discover a way to go on with your life. For as long as I can remember, I have always had a sense of social justice. I wonder if this incident was the beginning of my becoming someone who is able to fight on behalf of others. At least that would mean some good came of it.

After winning *New Faces* I was sought after; well, vaguely. Part of my prize was a season of cabaret at Lennons Hotel in Brisbane and as the support act to Johnny O'Keefe, Australian rock legend, at The Playroom Cabaret at Tallebudgera Creek on the Gold Coast. Can you imagine O'Keefe's audience liking this young girl doing show tunes? I felt, for the first time, what it feels like to 'die' on stage – good grounding for the future.

During my first year of teachers' college, I auditioned for and was cast in the College Players, a theatrical group run by Bryan Nason, a Brisbane theatre identity. They were doing a Brisbane season and a regional Queensland tour of *Salad Days* in the summer holidays.

What an adventure it was. We weren't paid, but expenses were covered. We had a highly decorated train carriage, which we slept in, with bunk beds and curtains, just like the carriage in the film *Some Like It Hot*. We hooked up to trains going our way. We would arrive in a town, put up the set, which would arrive by truck, while a couple of people shopped and cooked for everyone. Don't think any of it would pass HR these days, or any other rules of touring. I learnt so much, though; about acting and performing and discipline. We had such fun.

When we were in Charters Towers in Queensland, I got really drunk on bourbon and Coke at an after-show party. It is the only time in my life I have been drunk. I was so ill. The train trip the following day was excruciating. It took me a decade or more to even try to drink Coca Cola again. I couldn't even stand the smell of it. As for bourbon, I have never touched it again.

I continued with many singing gigs while at college, working on a regular basis with Bernard King, who acted as a kind of manager during those years. I first met Judi Connelli through Bernard. She was a few years older than me. Judi was to enjoy a great and long career, playing Mama Morton in our *Chicago*, amongst many other leading roles and successes.

Time seemed to move quickly. The arguments with my mother became worse and more frequent. She knew I was growing up, making friends away from her, and becoming independent. That might mean I would leave her. So the manipulation and intrigue were magnified. I had to walk on eggshells most of the time with Mother. I never knew when she was going to explode. I tried every day to placate her. It was exhausting. I realise that part of me – trying to smooth the waters, trying to not make people angry with me by attempting to be agreeable – has continued throughout my life, certainly with my relationships with men. That has not been a good thing. I tended to not give men boundaries as I was so frightened of losing them. Of course, that just gave them the licence to mistreat me emotionally.

Invariably, Mum used to cause a scene, pick a fight whenever I was looking forward to something. Usually on that day, as I was getting ready to go out (without her) she would create a huge scene so that it would spoil my excitement. Many a night, I would be covering up tears with makeup before I fled the house. When I was little, she could spoil things much more easily by locking me in a cupboard for a while. When I stopped screaming and was quiet and 'good' again, she would let me out. That didn't work when I got older. By then, my whole life was spent worrying about when the next axe would fall.

My interest in boys was ever growing, much to my mother's horror. The games began. It usually took just one hideous scene with my mother and most boys would never call again. One ex-boyfriend told me that in the middle of the night, when we were obviously asleep, Mum used to go in her dressing gown to a late-night coffee lounge he frequented and stand outside poking faces at him through the window, pushing her face against the glass. I was mortified as he asked, 'How is your mad mother?'

I didn't have the strength to answer him. Instead I hoped I could seek solace from my theatrical tribe.

3

Why Can't You Behave?

It is 1970. I buy my first golden retriever puppy and name her Gemima. I am working full-time with the Queensland Theatre Company.

Mum does not like that I am staying out late, dating boys, proving to be troublesome in her eyes. I have no doubt she is lonely, but I have my own life to live.

After a huge row, I take off with an overnight bag … just one night away from her is all I want. I run up the street to hail a cab. Mum runs after me and hails a cab to follow me. At a red light, I jump out of the taxi and run a block to another cab, just like in the movies. I lose her.

From what I hear later, she contacts every friend of mine, finally calling Carol Burns, a wonderful actress and friend who has taken me in for the night. I reluctantly come to the phone.

'I've killed the dog!'

'Okay. I'll come home.'

I know she hasn't killed the puppy, but I also know in that split second, she will say and do anything to win.

When I get home, Gemima is lapping some warm milk.

'Look at her. She's such a good puppy,' she says.

'You won't leave me again, will you?'

ॐ

I graduated teachers' college at the end of 1969. I was happy enough, but didn't really want to be a teacher. I needed to be on the stage.

I was placed at Woodridge State School, with Grade Two. I hadn't ever imagined teaching infants. At college, there were students who had specialised in infant school. I felt more at ease with older children. I had done well at college, except for failing sewing as I refused to finish my sampler. I thought it was stupid, sewing rows of different stitches ... why? So the teacher failed me. This did not please my mother, who had made all my clothes and couldn't understand my lack of interest in sewing. When I was at high school, Mum had sent me to a sewing class on a Tuesday night with Maureen King, who was my hearing-impaired next-door neighbour and friend. It was fun, but more so because the teacher made lovely cakes for each class. Mum had no idea I was only going for the cakes. I did attend for a year, but didn't retain much as my interest in sewing was zero. Mind you, over the last few years, I have made needlepoint cushions and handmade quilts for our home. Mother would be surprised.

So, there I was, getting lifts to Woodridge each day, doing my best, but longing for a way out. Then, when I heard that a brand new professional theatre company was starting up, I jumped at the chance. I remember turning up for the audition, with my obligatory Shakespearean monologue and a song in tow. I probably would not have been successful if they weren't to include a musical in their first season. My monologue was less than ordinary. However, my singing voice rang out on that stage and I knew I'd aced it.

I ended up resigning from teaching after six weeks.

Alan Edwards, the newly appointed artistic director of Queensland Theatre Company was an English director and actor. He created a real 'family' atmosphere, led acting classes, directed, mentored and was altogether a funny, generous colleague. I stayed with the company for two years and have returned over the years many times. This was my real grounding in theatre. It felt like I'd found the place for me. It felt like home.

It was Murray Foy, who was in that first repertory company with me, who told me about what to say to yourself to settle the nerves, while standing in the wings before your first entrance: 'I am beautiful. I am talented. I have a secret.' Then, you walk on with your secret about to burst. I have used it many times and have advised others of it.

The first show I appeared in was my first Australian musical, *A Rum Do*, which was about Governor Macquarie and the Rum Rebellion in the early days of the British colony of New South Wales. I played an innkeeper called Sadie, who sang a kind of 'oompahpah' number in Act One, 'Do Me a Favour'.

We did a season at the SGIO Theatre in 1970, attended (well, Act Two, at least) by the Queen, Prince Philip and Princess Anne. I will never forget, at the obligatory line-up with the royals after the play, how beautiful the young princess's skin was, so fine and flawless, almost translucent.

We then toured regional Queensland on an Arts Council bus. A step up from the College Players, but it was still an adventure. Sometimes, we were billeted, sometimes we were in hotels and, of course, we received a living allowance, so we could save some money. The show itself had its moments, but the lyrics I found awkward at times. This is a sample of the fast and clunky lyrics in my number.

Every time you lecture me on what I mustn't do
I'll shout out the battle cry of freedom
Do me a favour and let me be.

Even so, it was a success. It was the first of many new Australian musicals I have appeared in – I think sixteen at last count – which I believe is more than anyone else, ever. It has always been important to me to be a part of the creation of new works. It continues to be.

The following year, 1971, was my fullest year at QTC, rehearsing by day, playing by night, plus matinees. We toured the state with *She Stoops to Conquer* and *Oh, What a Lovely War* and we toured Queensland, New South Wales and the ACT with *The Legend of King O'Malley*, another Australian musical. Of course, our opening night in Canberra saw many politicians and John Gorton, former prime minister, in attendance, as the show was a raucous look at a very interesting time in Australian politics. I felt happy and safe, within the embrace of my tribe.

Then, in 1972, I played Mrs Squeezum, in *Lock Up Your Daughters* for the company. It was to be my last show with QTC until 1976, as I married and moved to Sydney straight after. Geoffrey Rush played the Town Crier and was petrified about opening the show each performance with a solo, as he suffered from nerves and was not at ease with his singing voice. He did relax and improve as the season progressed.

I met my first husband, Alan Wylie, an actor from Perth, during *Oh, What a Lovely War*. Surprise, surprise, Mum did not like Alan. She tolerated him after we were married, when she'd come to visit us to see me in a show. She never said anything complimentary to me about any of my performances. Nothing ... ever. Except once. I can't recall which show it was, but Mum always stayed in her seat at interval. Otherwise she thought she might miss something. This one time, she told me afterwards the woman behind her tapped her on the shoulder and asked, out of the blue, if I was her daughter. A little unbelievable, I thought. Why would that happen? Then the woman went on.

'Isn't she wonderful?'

'Well, I had to agree,' Mum said, begrudgingly. That was the only time I remember receiving any praise from her.

I stayed in caravan parks, when not billeted, on one of those QTC tours, to save money to send my parents to New Guinea to visit my brother Ralph, who had been living there with his family. Dad was thankful. I trust Mum was. She never said. She was impossible to please.

The regular beatings of my mother continued. I never confronted Dad about it, not even several years later, after Mum had died. How on earth would I do that anyway? How could I broach it with him? It remained a nasty secret that hovered over us all. I felt helpless and I never ever spoke of it. Dad hit Mum only when he was drunk. Did the drink give him Dutch courage? Was he insecure from his own rather jagged upbringing? Did he feel inferior to others? Did his lack of a formal education colour his life? I guess a combination of all those things. Dad was soft and kind and caring ... most of the time. When Mr Hyde appeared, everything blew up and the house turned into a house of despair. My stomach is churning writing these words. These experiences don't fade with time.

4

And Her Mother Came Too

During *A Rum Do, my first show with QTC in 1970, I meet, and start seeing Terry Bader, an actor from Sydney, who is in the cast. He is my first real boyfriend. Terry is to star in the play,* Philadelphia, Here I Come, *just after the tour of* A Rum Do. *His parents, Bill and Lynne, are coming up from Sydney for the opening and I am to meet them and sit with them.*

When my mother hears this, I am sure she thinks this is a sign she is about to lose me. Meeting the parents cannot be good.

On the opening night, as I am at home dressing to the nines, there is a huge row. Mum swears she will come in and ruin my evening.

I plead with Dad to try to get her to stay home, as I know from experience she has dreamt up a devastating scene to play out.

I have a splitting headache as the cab arrives at the theatre and I meet Bill and Lynne. The play is wonderful. I am nervous. At interval, I search the bar area and the foyer but cannot see her. Perhaps she is home, tucked up in bed.

After the second act and the huge ovation, we walk down the stairs to the foyer and there is mum in her dressing gown, with rollers in her hair, playing her best role, the destroyer. She shouts, 'Do you know what your son is doing to my daughter? He's fucking her! That's what he's doing. He's fucking her!'

I don't notice the reactions from the audience, who are pouring into the foyer.

There is a loud buzzing in my head. I am so embarrassed. I am panicked. I scream.
Lynne tries to hold me. I push her away and run out of the theatre, down the lane
to stage door and backstage to Terry's dressing room. I am inconsolable. Bill and
Lynne are there by now. Mother has disappeared. She has done her job. I am sure she
is pleased with herself. What a way to meet these lovely people!

❧

I was twenty. Mum often talked about getting the police if I attempted to run
away. I believed her.

My relationship with Terry didn't last, although we did attempt a few
reconciliations over the next few years. Our lives went in different directions,
but I always think fondly of him and all his family, whom I came to know
well over the years. I worked and became friends with his sister, Valerie,
on *No, No, Nanette*, with brother, Stephen Thomas, in *Ned Kelly*, another
Australian musical premiere, and brother, Michael, who became a stage
manager with Sydney Theatre Company. Happily, I have had an ongoing
relationship with all of the Baders.

The following year, 1971, I met my first husband, Alan Wylie. I don't
really think I loved him. I thought I did. Well, it feels the same, thinking you
do. It is only later, when you realise you don't, that you think, 'Oh it mustn't
have been love.'

We had a little over two years together. Alan stood up to my mother. No
man ever had done that. Also, he was a way out. I think I married him to get
away from my mother.

She was not pleased. Most of all, she hated that we were moving to
Sydney the day after the wedding and taking Gemima. Mother loved dogs.
I always have as well. I love dogs more than people. You know where you
stand with a dog.

The wedding took place on 9 April 1972. Alan's mother arrived from
Perth and came to dinner at my parents' house two nights before. Of course
there was a scene. Mum suddenly announced she was going to kill herself,
took a huge carving knife out of the kitchen drawer, making sure everyone
saw her do it, and left the dining room.

Alan's mother was a little hysterical. 'She's got a huge knife!'

No-one moved. We knew the histrionics very well. All conversation ceased. We continued to eat. Things went strangely quiet. Some time passed. Eventually, Mum returned, put the knife back in the kitchen drawer and served dessert. Nothing more was said about the episode.

On the day of the ceremony, Mum looked like hell. In all the photos, she looks as if the world is ending. Weddings should be a wonderful memory of a wonderful day. Not this one. I was distraught for most of the day. I knew my mother was in a desperate state at the thought of losing me and I was half waiting for a big scene. What would she do? What could she do? The last ditch attempt at stopping the wedding had been the false suicide threat. Now we were married and I was leaving. This was real. Surely that is why Mother looked like she did. I had a splitting headache for the whole day. Mum kept following me around at the catered party in our garden saying, 'He's got you where he wants you now. He's going to take you home and fuck you!'

At least she was consistent.

5

Easy to Be Hard

It is that time between waking and sleeping, when you're not sure what is real. Is it a dream? Are you awake?

'If she's blue, she's dead.'

That's what I hear my brother Ray saying on the hallway phone, just outside my bedroom. We are back in 1970. I am finished for that year at QTC till my contract the following year. Suddenly, my mother is sitting on my bed.

'Michelle is dead. Noel hit her.'

My brother Noel and his wife have a daughter who is five. His wife's sister from Sydney has some issues, so her three-year old daughter, Michelle, comes to live with them. Who knows what has happened? I hear from Mum that Noel, while drunk, arguing with his wife, gets angry, punches Michelle in the stomach in a drunken rage. He is up all night holding her, trying to settle her, pacing with her in his arms, too scared to take her to the hospital because he knows they'll notice the bruises and ask questions.

He bolts.

His wife is on the phone to my brother Ray, who is visiting from New Zealand, where he has lived with his wife and small children for a few years.

I blurt out that I never want to see or speak with Noel again. Almost as I say this, Noel arrives, stands at the front door, looking like hell, a broken man.

'What am I going to do Mum?' he asks pathetically with tears in his eyes.

Mum puts on the kettle. (Cups of tea fix everything.)

At that moment, Noel is not the person I vowed never to speak to again. He is simply my brother, my brother who had such promise. He made comics as a teenager. Wrote the stories, created the characters, drew all the pictures. He had real talent. If only he had kept that dream alive. I suppose he didn't know how.

Mum says he fell in with a bad crowd; her answer for everything.

Noel asks me for money so he can run. I say that is not the answer. I go to help Mum in the kitchen. We bring back the tea, but Noel is gone.

We hear the police pick him up and beat the shit out of him a few hours later.

Dad sold his car to pay for a barrister for the hearing. After that, Noel had a public defender. I went once to the hearing, where the lawyer questioned several doctors about the bruising on the poor little girl's tummy. The lawyer proved a case for reasonable doubt; that the bruises on Michelle's body could have been caused by falling off a swing a few days earlier, which apparently she had done. Noel had been charged with murder, but he was convicted of manslaughter.

Ralph, my eldest brother, was the only one who visited Noel in jail. I admire him for that. Ray fled back to New Zealand. Leigh had never got on with Noel, so there was no question of his visiting. Noel was the black sheep. I always had a soft spot for him. I can't explain why. I guess of all my brothers, he was the one who was very supportive of my dreams. After his conviction, I continued to visit him in jail. It always felt surreal, going to a prison.

The judge on the case was a friend from school's father, Walter Campbell, who later became Sir Walter Campbell, a governor of Queensland. This whole thing was an awful, awful episode for our family. The press went to town. Who knows what Noel was confronted with in prison? Child killers are not given an easy time.

Since that time, I have always watched the news and thought about everyday people, who end up in prison after making the wrong, split-second decision and ruin their lives in that moment. Most people are in prison because of a bad choice made in an irrational moment. There aren't many serial killers or psychopaths, thankfully; rather, regular folk, who for some reason, on a particular day, commit a crime. I often say out loud while watching a news report, 'You have just ruined your life.'

Noel served three years of a five-year sentence for manslaughter. He never recovered. Never forgave himself. Started drinking again to dull the pain. I saw him a few times after his release. By then, I was not home in Brisbane much, living in Melbourne, then Sydney, and very busy with my career.

Fast-forward a decade or so. Mum died in September 1982. I was living in Sydney with Bill Shanahan, my agent and great friend, and Kristian Fredrikson, friend and famous theatre designer. I had just been to the cinema to see *Nine to Five* and was watching Princess Grace's funeral on TV, while Bill was preparing dinner. It was a Sunday. There was a knock at the door. Bill answered. It was the police to tell me there was bad news about my mother and I was to call my brother Ralph's house.

I knew she was dead. I remember panicking and saying that if I never called, it wouldn't be true. Mum was the first person I ever knew who died. Bill called for me and told me the news that Mum and Dad had been visiting Ralph and family on the Sunshine Coast. She had started ranting, saying she was dying. She had done that to great effect over the years during arguments, to gain sympathy if she was losing. So they didn't take much notice. This time it was real. Heart attack.

We all returned for the funeral.

Noel was embarrassed about attending. He hadn't seen many of the aunts, uncles and cousins since his trial and incarceration. He had kept to himself, in and out of dead-end jobs, living some sort of half-life. Finally, Noel announced, 'I can't go, Dad. I will embarrass the family. No-one will want me there.'

I will never forget my father's response. I loved him for it. 'You will come to the funeral, son, and you will sit next to me.'

Makes me cry.

I didn't go in to see the open casket. Couldn't. I did catch a long-distanced glimpse of Dad, holding Mum's hand, kneeling at the casket and crying. The image is emblazoned across my brain. He must have loved her. I had never understood that. Once, I saw them kissing in the kitchen in the house at Annerley. I remember thinking that I had not seen any spark between them before that kiss. Dad was distraught at Mum's funeral, as was I. The boys looked as if they weren't there.

I was sad that Mum was not buried with her 'old teeth'. Mum had dentures. For as long as I can remember, she had lived with her top denture, which had broken in half. Each week, as it became unstuck, she would sit in the kitchen and glue it together with Tarzan's Grip. It only ever lasted a week before breaking again. After years and years of trying to get her to go to a dentist, she capitulated, only a few months before her death. She received a top-notch upper denture, which she never liked. Found uncomfortable. Never even liked the look of it. She had kept the old broken one. I do wish Dad had insisted she be buried with that old, comfortable one. We could have got the Tarzan's Grip out one last time for the occasion.

The day before Mum's funeral a neighbour had invited us over for afternoon tea. Noel declined as he was hungover and decided to take a nap. We weren't there long when we received a frantic phone call from Noel. 'You've gotta come back. I saw Mum standing at the end of the bed.'

Well, you know what they say about drunks and animals being able to see ghosts.

We went home, where Noel told us about Mum standing at the end of the bed as he awoke from his nap. 'She was holding this bloke's hand. He had long red hair and he was wearing a toga! Mum hates foreigners.'

A few years later, when Bill Shanahan, my wonderful manager, had secured me a cabaret season in Newcastle during a down time, one of the band members had a psychic grandmother. I was bored by day, so agreed to a psychic reading.

I walked into this woman's house and as soon as she saw me, she announced, 'Your mother is fine. She is with a guide.'

Of course, I started 'humping crying'. She went on. 'Her guide is a Scottish laird. He has long red hair and he's wearing a kilt.'

Suddenly, a shiver went through me. I asked if it could be a toga that he was wearing.

'Well, yes, I thought that at first. But it is definitely a kilt!'

Goosebumps!

The only other time I recall any sort of ghost encounter (and I am a sceptic) happened years later at my Petersham house in Sydney. I was alone. I was asleep; well, waking up. I felt a cold, damp hand sweep across my forehead. It was unmistakable. I opened my eyes to see a man in a long cloak, a man from another time, standing over me and staring. I knew in that instant, he was not a good person. The vibe was very negative. Suddenly, he vanished.

I got up, put the kettle on and talked some sense to myself. 'Don't be ridiculous. You were dreaming,' I said out loud. I forgot about it.

A couple of years later, a good friend was staying in the guest room, looking after my darling dogs, Tiger and Teddy, while I was overseas. I called Geoffrey to see how the dogs were, how everything was going.

He said all was fine except he'd had a strange encounter the day before. He had been asleep. It was early morning. He opened his eyes to see a man in a long cloak, a man from another time, standing in the doorway looking at him. He said that he felt a negative vibe. The man was not a good man. Then, suddenly, the man vanished.

As he was telling me, I knew everything he was about to say.

More goosebumps.

6

I Want to Be Happy

Freddie Carpenter, the director of No, No, Nanette is a flamboyant, old-fashioned queen with a bad toupee, who is at times charming, but can turn like a black snake. We open in Melbourne in 1972 and play beyond a year there. We are a smash. This is the era that sees J. C. Williamson's join forces with Edgley's to become Williamson-Edgley Theatres. It is costume parade day, the time the producers and the director and choreographer see all the costumes before technical rehearsals at the theatre. Things may need tweaking. Each of the principals comes out on stage, with all the executives – future employers, mind – sitting in the audience, with Freddie fussing about on stage.

It is my turn. I play Betty from Boston and have some lovely costumes. Freddie circles me. Then, he looks out at everyone in the audience and says, referring to me with his hands flourishing for dramatic effect, 'I mean how can you make someone who looks like this look good?'

I manage to hold it together until I get to my dressing room, as the tears start to flow. I am 21. My friends and colleagues in the show reassure me.

It does not stop there. During previews, Freddie sometimes stands in the wings, watching from prompt corner. He tells me over and over again that I will never get anywhere in the theatre looking as I do. All I can think is he is referring to my big breasts. Perhaps he thinks I look altogether hideous. Who can tell?

'If you want a career, you should spare no expense!'
At all other times, he is nice to me. Whoop de doo!

My new husband Alan and I left Brisbane on 10 April 1972, the day after the wedding. We moved to Surry Hills in Sydney. That week, I auditioned for Betty Pounder, choreographer, and Brian Buggy, musical director, for *No, No, Nanette*. I got the part.

My opening night note from Pounder said that she was glad they had waited for me and that I would go a long way with my great talent. (Much better than, 'You're a lovely little girl with a pretty smile' …) I still have Betty Pounder's note.

I believe someone else was all but cast as Betty, until they reconsidered and cast me after my audition. I talked my way into an agency, June Cann Management in Sydney. I am thankful to June for taking on an unknown. She must have seen something in me.

I moved to Melbourne to start rehearsals without Alan, who arrived a few weeks later, having driven down with Gemima. I moved in with Lesley and Will Deumer, at a rather well-known actors' digs in Andrew Street, Windsor. It was an enclave. Over the next few years, I lived in four different flats/cottages there.

The show starred Cyd Charisse, with Bobby Limb playing her husband, and Jill Perryman, with Paul Wallace (Broadway and film Tulsa in *Gypsy*) as her husband. The juvenile leads were Rosalie Howard as Nanette, with Jon Sidney and Rosie Sturgess, Pamela Gibbons, Anne Grigg and I rounding out the principal players.

After more than a year of the show, Yvonne De Carlo replaced Cyd. This was for the end of the Melbourne run, the Sydney season, and the tour. At the same time, Kevan Johnston, Jill Perryman's husband, took over from Paul Wallace.

Cyd was a lovely, if an intensely shy person. If you went to her and struck up a conversation, she was very responsive, collegiate and friendly. Otherwise, she kept to herself, preferring to spend time with her friend and personal assistant, Hortense. It was easy to imagine that Cyd was unfriendly, which some of the ensemble did. She was very friendly, but she was just not one of the gang, I guess. A specialty dance sequence was added for her in Act One, so audiences could glimpse those famous legs for themselves.

Paul Wallace was a little crazy, but I liked him. I saw him out the front of the theatre measuring his name on the billboard one day to check that the size of the print was the one agreed in his contract. Mind you, I do understand billing upsets. It was other things, like telling us about his expertise in birthing puppies and how you must throw them against a brick wall to start them breathing! Also, it was obvious he was gay, but it was never talked about. One didn't in some circles. Rather sad, I thought. He was, however, a great colleague. I wish I had quizzed him more about Ethel Merman and Rosalind Russell, two of my heroes.

I saw Cyd Charisse years and years later at a Foxtel dinner, not too long before she died. I didn't know if she would remember me. Why would she? As I approached her table and said I had been in *No, No, Nanette* with her, she immediately said, 'Geraldine! Are you still singing, with that wonderful voice?'

I was touched that she had remembered me.

I recall our darling golden retriever Gemima having nine beautiful puppies during a matinee one day. Alan was in attendance with her, while Gail Esler, one of our stage managers was on the phone to Alan, informing me as I exited after each scene, just how many puppies had been born. Alan didn't throw them against a brick wall to make them breathe, funnily enough.

Gemima was a wonderful mother. We kept one of her sons, Toby, and since then, I have always had two dogs. I think it is better for them, and more than double the love. We gave one of the boys to Mum and Dad. Boris lived a long and happy life.

Yvonne, unlike Cyd, was absolutely one of the gang – and naughty. They interpolated 'More Than You Know' into Act One for her, instead of the dance sequence. She had come to Australia after hocking her furs. She needed money as she had recently lost a huge lawsuit. Fascinating, that as the first 'Carlotta' in *Follies*, some of those lyrics in 'I'm Still Here' are actually about her life.

Yvonne liked motorbikes, and bikers. She was given a huge motorbike as a promotion. Don't know if she ever rode it, but she took it up in the elevator to her suite in the hotel. It lived in the hallway just outside her door.

I remember one day before her first entrance, she climbed the fly tower ladder and as Sue Nattrass, stage director extraordinaire, urged her in whispers to come down for her entrance, she kept shaking her head, as stage crew began the climb to get to her. Eventually, she came down in floods of laughter, with seconds to spare.

Another time, Rosalie (Nanette) had taken Yvonne to a clairvoyant, who had told her to be very careful on a certain upcoming date. Yvonne got it in her mind she would be shot from the audience; a stretch, I know. Apparently, she had done some favours for the Mob, and she imagined, as the date talked about was a matinee day, that something dire was about to happen. The whole day, Yvonne kept hiding behind others on stage. In every number, she pushed dancers in front of her so they'd take the bullet for her. It was very amusing. We got through the day, somehow, without incident. God only knows what the audience thought about hardly getting a glimpse of the leading lady.

I recall being at a dinner with all the principals where Yvonne talked about Picasso coming to her home for a dinner party once and sketching on all of her dinnerware. Jill Perryman asked what she had done with the plates, as that could solve any future debt issues, and more.

'Oh, I think I threw them out in a house move.'

This was one of the fabulous parties at Betty Pounder's wonderful home in Alexandra Avenue, on the river. I remember being offered another glass of champagne by someone and Pounder saying, 'Geraldine, if you have another drink, I'll take you off my star list.'

Think I said 'no'.

It was such a big show that we had the luxury of pit singers to enhance the sound in all dance and chorus numbers. One of the pit singers, who shall remain nameless, was disliked by most of the cast.

One day, for instance, he was really late for rehearsal and I mean hours late. As he strolled in to a waiting, furious Sue Nattrass and John Robertson, our stage manager, he said, 'Sorry I'm late. My baby died.'

Sue immediately told him to go home, that she would call later, check if there were something we could do. I think we took up a collection.

Turns out he wasn't married, had no partner or child, he'd just slept in. This was the first of many lies. One of the big ones was that he had been diagnosed with a terminal illness and had a year to live. I guess he needed sympathy that day for some reason.

Most of us forgot that lie as many more were blurted out during the season, and it all became a 'boy who cried wolf' story.

Sometime later, we were playing in Auckland at St James Theatre, when Teddy Ashton, another pit singer was seen fussing and tidying up this person's dressing-room station, polishing his mirror, rearranging things to look lovely. At that moment, our pathological liar walked in and said, 'What are you doing, Teddy? You've never liked me. Why are you being so nice? Why are you tidying up my place in the dressing room?'

'Exactly one year ago today, you told us all you had a year to live. I just want to make sure your last day on earth is happy!'

And as only an old-fashioned queen can, Teddy turned on his heels and swept out.

Actually, Teddy came to a sad end. Some years later, he had stopped getting work in the industry and had taken a job in a department store, in retail. There was a scandal about some goods or money missing and Teddy found himself convicted and jailed. Turned out Teddy liked jail. He liked the routine, the rules, the meals at the same time each day, and the fact that he didn't have to worry about money. When the time came for his release, he begged the authorities to be able to stay. Of course, that was not possible.

He did not cope with being on the outside and he killed himself not long after. It was such a shock. This was a sad end to a fabulous singer and raconteur, a wonderful, funny colleague, whom I had first met when I was just seventeen in Brisbane, when he had been part of the original company of *Fiddler On the Roof.*

I understudied Jill Perryman in *No, No, Nanette,* the only time in my career that I have understudied. I never went on, but I did do the final dress rehearsal in Sydney, at the Regent Theatre. Jill was resting from a nasty cold. As it happened, all the producers watched that rehearsal. Timing is everything. I believe I did a good job but I was far too young to play Lucille. I did receive compliments from management, however.

After the Sydney season, we went to Auckland. We were to play Auckland, Wellington and Christchurch, with a small break in between Auckland and Wellington so that some people could get home to see partners if they wished. Things changed and it was decided we'd play Palmerston North before Wellington and forego the proposed Christchurch season. I was livid, as I had planned to go home for that break. So I resigned. I left near the end of Auckland, with many people saying that I would never work again. I was concerned about that but did it anyway.

I wish, in a way, that I had stayed, as the Palmerston North season was a treat, I heard, and I say that ironically. They had reduced the orchestra to cut costs, so that the pit singers sang extra harmonies, to fill out the sound, literally becoming a part of the orchestra. One day, one of the players in the orchestra had a breakdown during Act One of the show. She began laughing hysterically during numbers. When the conductor tapped his baton at her to stop, she tapped back at him and laughed even more loudly. Finally, she started ripping up her score, page by page, and throwing the pages high into the air defiantly. She was taken away at interval. I do wish I had seen it.

As it turned out, J. C. Williamson's asked me to do their next show, *A Little Night Music*, which was to open the newly built Her Majesty's Theatre in Sydney, on 30 November 1973, and more importantly, it was to open up my future career. They needed a girl with a big voice (this was before body microphones) to play Petra and to sing the Act Two show stopper 'The Miller's Son'. I was that girl. Guess I had survived Betty Pounder's star list.

Rehearsals were exciting in my first of many Sondheim shows. It was the original, divine Harold Prince production, directed in Australia by George Martin. I recall well the opening night in Sydney and the huge ovation I received. More importantly, the great Australian soprano, Gladys Moncrieff, not long before her passing, was at that opening and I was introduced to her at the party after the show. What a wonderful thing to happen to a young girl.

The show starred Taina Elg, former MGM starlet, with Bruce Barry, Jill Perryman, David Gilchrist, Anne Grigg and Tim Page, with the fabulous comedienne, Anna Russell as Madame Armfeldt.

Taina was a wonderful Desirée, but Jill as Charlotte was an audience favourite. She was a great and very funny Charlotte. It is a wonderful role. I believe it was simply that Taina was not as well known here in Australia, and the fact that her performance was understated, that led to the balance being a little off and Jill running away with the reviews. In fact, having seen the show a number of times over the years and having done the show now three times, twice as Desirée, there is a fine balance a production should strike. In my opinion, if Charlotte overshadows Desirée, there is something wrong with the production.

Also in the cast was Bartholomew John, who, more than a decade later, would play my Bill Sykes in *Oliver!*, and Wayne Harrison, who had been in *No, No, Nanette* and would go on to become a theatre director and producer of note.

Anna Russell, who played Desirée's mother, a former courtesan, was not available for six weeks of the Sydney season, as she had an overseas concert tour planned. So it was decided to use Doris Fitton, a Sydney theatre identity, who had run the Independent Theatre in North Sydney for many years, to replace her for those six weeks.

This decision turned out to be a disaster. After weeks studying and rehearsing with stage management and understudies, we were all called in to do a final run with Doris, a costume run for her. She was opening the following week.

Doris had not retained one word … and it is a big part!

We were in shock. What was the company going to do? Well, it was early days of body microphone technology. Our stage manager, Peter Wagner, suggested an earpiece for Miss Fitton. He would feed every line to her from prompt corner.

It was six weeks of hell. For instance, in a scene in Act Two with her granddaughter, Fredrika, Madame talks of an ex-lover. She says, 'He gave me a wooden ring.' Then the speech continues. Well, she would be fed the line, but she would say, 'He … [pause] … ring.'

It happened all the time as actors glazed over, wondering if the audience understood anything about the story, as poor Miss Fitton said every fourth word in any sentence. Most nights, 'Liaisons', her wonderful number in Act One, was a train wreck.

One night in particular was memorable. The marvellous dining scene in Act Two sees a sumptuously decorated dining table trucked on from the wings, with all major characters with their backs to the audience. Only Madame Armfeldt is facing the audience and she starts the scene. I was playing Petra, a maid, so I was holding a tray of glasses, as were Bart John and Wayne Harrison.

Nothing happened. Always in a moment like this on stage, you think an hour has passed. Time stands still and you hope the stage opens up so you can fall through into another world, or simply that you will die there one day. All the principals were willing Miss Fitton to begin the scene. The audience started coughing. This is never a good sign.

We realised, as Doris started banging her ear with her hand, that her earpiece had fallen out during the table's entrance. Like all good servants, Bart, Wayne and I started crawling around the stage looking for the earpiece. What must the audience have thought? Wayne found it and placed it in Miss Fitton's ear, trying not to appear too familiar as a lowly servant. At last, the scene could begin.

Many folk speak of Doris picking up radio frequencies from Deluxe Taxis and blurting out an address in the inner city for pick-up, but I fear that is an apocryphal story!

When Anna Russell returned to the show, we were overjoyed. She was fabulous in the role and such fun to be around.

Around the late 90s early 2000s, Anna returned to Australia to live full-time on the south coast of New South Wales after a stellar international career. She had been born and brought up in England, but had enjoyed a career on most continents, having spent a great deal of her life in Canada, where she had enjoyed a fabulous, ongoing career. But her adopted daughter lived in Australia and Anna had had many great times here with her concert career. In fact, her very last concert was at the Sydney Opera House.

My husband Brian and I visited her in Rosedale, on the beautiful south coast of New South Wales, not long before she died. She looked wonderful, with glowing skin and, though frail, her memory was like that of an elephant. I asked her if she had felt sad after her final concert in Sydney after such an amazing career. Anna said, 'Not at all. I took my makeup box down to the front of the Opera House boardwalk and dropped it into the harbour, thought, that's that, and went home.'

Her home on the south coast, which she shared with her daughter who was more like her carer and friend, was right on the water, facing onto a lovely beach. I asked her if she ever took a walk on the beach.

Anna said, a little crossly, and ever so grandly, 'I would, if someone would tell me where the beach is!'

We played Sydney, Brisbane (where we sold out!), Adelaide and Melbourne with *A Little Night Music*. Mum came to the opening in Brisbane, but, unsurprisingly, didn't say anything to me about my performance. I stayed at home for that Brisbane season. There were fewer fights with Mother, but they still occurred. She hated me staying out late. I was twenty-three years old.

Sometimes, it was easy to distract Mum from a confrontation. If I were to arrive at home in the early hours, all I needed to do was bring her chips and a burger as a late night treat. She was always awake, waiting. And she was always ready for a fight about where I'd been, who I'd been with, why I was so late. I could never creep in and simply go to bed. However, before she had a chance to yell, if I presented a late-night feast, we could share it in the kitchen and laugh and tell stories. She loved that.

Things seemed a little better between Mum and Dad during that trip. I wasn't at the house all the time, of course, but Mum was certainly calmer and Dad wasn't drinking so much. That could only be a good thing.

Then, it was on to Melbourne with the show. During the Melbourne season of *A Little Night Music*, one matinee day, Bruce Barry was singing 'Now', during which he undresses, takes his shoes off, and dresses into napping clothes. It is a fast, wordy, complex number. I was waiting in the wings to make an entrance straight after, when I heard him forget his lyrics. The music played on. He walked offstage. I yelled the lyrics out to him. But I know from experience that in the panic, you tend to go deaf to everything.

Honestly, he could have picked up the song in the middle and the audience would have been forgiving or none the wiser. And isn't it better to keep going, while attempting to hold on to your character?

Makes me think of a time during *The Ghost Train* years before at Queensland Theatre Company. In this particular part of the play all the characters are locked in the train station, so cannot leave the stage. One of our actors was ill that matinee (why is it always a matinee?) so he walked upstage, knelt down and quietly threw up in a corner, as we all took his lines for him, like the great ensemble we were. I had friends in the audience that day. They did not notice. They thought he was looking for clues. My point is, audiences usually accept most things as being a part of it all ... unless you come out of character and stop.

So, Bruce walked down to the front of the stage, signalled to the conductor, Noel Smith to stop. He then said to the audience, 'This is a very difficult song with very difficult lyrics. Let's take it from the top.'

This show was musical director and friend Michael Tyack's first show. He played second keyboard in Melbourne and recalls this incident as clearly as I do. I had never experienced anything like that. All belief in Bruce as his character, Fredrik, flew out the window.

He began again after having to re-dress, with the help of his dresser. Minutes passed with nothing happening, except for the odd cough from the audience, as Bruce got back in his costume.

Of course, when he began again, you guessed it. He got to the same part of the song and dried again. Stopped the orchestra again. Said, 'We'll start again. I want to get this right.'

Third time he nailed it and we went on with the play.

Taina Elg and I became great friends. Every time I visited New York over the following years, we caught up. We spoke many times on the phone in between visits.

I remember a party at someone's house during the Sydney season. I couldn't find my husband, Alan. Someone said they thought he was on the roof terrace. I climbed the stairs to find Alan kissing Taina on the roof. I was shocked, naturally, but I recall not feeling too badly about it. I guess later it forced me to think about my feelings for Alan and where I stood on that.

Taina, of course, was distraught. She asked me to forgive a silly old woman! (She was only in her forties.) There was no question that I wouldn't. All remained fine between us.

During one of my trips to New York years later, when Taina was playing the mother in the original Broadway cast of *Nine*, she got me house seats for a performance. I adored Tommy Tune and his tremendous talent as both performer and director. This production and his production of *Grand Hotel* are two of the most memorable and brilliant musical theatre performances I have ever seen.

Taina said that the whole cast of *Nine* was in love with Tommy. I can understand that. I did meet him some years later in Sydney when he did a workshop of a proposed new version of *Easter Parade*, which never happened.

One day in New York, on one of Taina's days off, we met for a coffee and a long walk through Central Park. At one point, I noticed an old woman, a very ordinary old woman, with dark glasses, a hat, and wearing a boxy suit (probably Chanel, with hindsight) standing beside me. Taina grabbed me, pulled me aside and whispered, 'That is Greta Garbo.'

She took a walk in the park every day, apparently. I would never have known her. To this day, I am really chuffed that one of the greatest stars and beauties the world has ever laid eyes on was, for a few minutes, standing right there beside me.

As Taina grew older she became the most beautiful, older version of herself. She chose not to have any face work done. I believe that is the next frontier, making it more than okay for a woman to grow old gracefully on stage and screen, if she chooses. After all, men are allowed to look older, while still considered sexy and interesting. Why this is not a feminist issue I don't know. Is it big studios and producers who insist on women looking 'young'? Or is it young women themselves, who insist on so many fillers, so much botox, so much building up of lips to the 'Daffy Duck' status, so many facelifts, that they look like aliens, that there is often little to no character in a woman's face? It'll be interesting to see how it all plays out in the next few years. Personally, I think a little tweak here and there is fine and I wouldn't mind all the major face work if people simply looked younger, instead of looking pulled and stretched and weird, with old hands.

I have many wonderful memories of that tour of *A Little Night Music*, not so of my life. I was unhappy in my marriage two years down the track. The 'kissing' incident had not helped. I had an affair during the Brisbane run of the show. No wonder mother was suspicious of my comings and goings.

When we closed in Brisbane, I remember Alan picking me up at the airport for a few days home in Sydney, before the Melbourne season.

Alan said as I walked towards him, 'You've had an affair, haven't you?'

'Yes'

'You're going to leave me.'

'Yes.'

And that was that.

7

How Much of the Dream Comes True?

It is 1975. I am living in Melbourne, doing a television series, The Box. I am a regular character in this show about a TV station. I haven't sung for a while. Jon Finlayson, a well-known actor, producer, director and writer comes up with an idea for a cabaret show called, The Glitter Sisters, which is based loosely on the Andrew Sisters. Five women, in this case, singing harmonies, duets and solos from the Second World War years. We are a hit. I am tired, but it fits in with my filming commitments. There is talk of it continuing and touring. I am not interested in that. Also, filming the television show prevents touring. Jon comes up with another idea, The Tarnish Brothers and Virginia Creeper in Close Harmony, four boys and me. Ever the ambitious young thing, I leap at this. It bombs.

We play these shows at the Whitehorse Hotel in Nunawading, a suburb of Melbourne. It is a vast room. It seats hundreds. With Tarnish Brothers, there is one night we play to three … one table of two and one man on his own. At interval, the table of two leaves.

Postscript: In 2019, I am doing a concert and a woman walks up to me after the show and announces that she is one of the table of two who left that night. I am so shocked that she freely admits this to me that I am struck dumb.

People think they can say anything to you and you won't get hurt. Reminds me of the time I am staying at the Regency in Melbourne. A man walks up to me as I am getting in the lift. He says, 'Aren't you Geraldine Turner?'

'Well, yes I am.'

I imagine he will go on to say, 'You're my favourite actress,' or 'I love your work.' Instead, he blurts out, 'You've stacked on the beef, haven't you?'

I look blank as the elevator doors close.

Lesson is, don't ever get ahead of yourself.

At the end of 1974, I moved to Melbourne. Sadly for me, Alan kept the dogs, soon moved on and moved in with our bridesmaid, and they have been together ever since. I moved into Andrew Street again and later moved to a fabulous share flat in Toorak with Sue O'Connor, who had been in *No, No, Nanette* with me. The rest of that year, I appeared in a couple of guest roles in Crawfords dramas, *Homicide* and *Division 4*.

In 1975, I appeared in that long-running role in *The Box*. During my time on the show, we turned to colour TV in Australia, and I felt a real part of history. In those days, each week, the actors were handed piles of taxi dockets. These were supposed to be to get us to and from rehearsal and filming days. Many of us abused this system by going to boutiques, trying on clothes while the taxi waited, or doing our supermarketing on the way home from rehearsals and getting the taxi to wait. I think, with hindsight, Crawford Productions placed a little too much trust in us. They were happy times. We were naughty.

Then, of course, those two cabaret seasons happened around then. My character in *The Box* was written out, after more than a year, to go to Fiji to train an All Black soccer team. Where do they come up with these story lines?

After that, I was cast as Doreen, in the musical version of *The Sentimental Bloke* by Nancy Brown and Albert Arlen for ABC television. What a joy, playing opposite Graeme Blundell, with Nancye Hayes (first time we worked together) and Jimmy Hannan. I remember being at Nancy Brown and Albert Arlen's gorgeous home in Watsons Bay in Sydney, with Albert playing through the score and chatting through the concepts for this TV version.

Alan Burke, who had been one of the writers of famous Australian musical *Lola Montez*, directed the show. We became great friends and worked together many times over the years. In fact, years later I sang a song from his and Peter Stannard's musical version of *The Harp in the South* as a tribute to him at his memorial service.

The Sentimental Bloke was a time when productions were 'in house' and the ABC had full costume departments and set designers on staff – and real budgets! It was a quaint and interesting iteration of the piece, with cartoon-like, colourful sets, some marvellous choreography by Joe Latona and terrific performances from the major principals, with Jon Finlayson, and Anne Phelan and Laine Lamont, who had both been in *The Glitter Sisters* with me. Now, they are both sadly gone, as are Jon, and Betty Ann Bobbitt, who was also in *The Glitter Sisters*.

I remember clearly being cocooned in a recording studio all day in Melbourne, where we shot the piece. We sang each song 'live' to a prerecorded orchestra on filming days, but were present, while the orchestra recorded the score, to sing along to get the musical timings right. When you're in a studio, the world outside may as well not exist as you focus on the task at hand. So, you can imagine how shocked we were to emerge after a full day's recording to find out that the Whitlam Government had been sacked.

I had moved back to the biggest apartment at Andrew Street by then, with my brother Leigh and his second wife, Nerida.

I recall a visit home to Brisbane some years earlier, and a trip I took with my parents, Leigh and Nerida to see my eldest brother, Ralph, his wife and two very young boys on the Sunshine Coast of Queensland. Unsurprisingly, there was a big fight, probably about Dad lending Leigh some money years earlier. I say that, as it was a regular thorn in the side for my brothers, the fact that Leigh had not paid the money back to Dad. Ralph was an alcoholic and became very unreasonable when on a binge. Jewel, his wife, believed that if you had brown eyes like me, you must have 'black blood' in you.

Even if there were an ounce of truth in that, so what? Unbelievable! She was thankful her sons had blue eyes. Racism was ever present in Queensland in those days; still is, to my horror, in certain circles.

I have blocked out which one of them grabbed it. All I know is the shotgun suddenly appeared. Things escalated. Didn't know if it was loaded. I do remember grabbing Ralph's two young boys, running out to the car and hiding them under the seats as tempers flared and I waited to hear a gunshot. It was tense to say the least. The shouting went on and on. I was scared.

Dad managed to calm things down. God knows how, as everyone was screaming abuse. Dad was good at breaking up tension. He had to use all his skills that day. I was always sad that Dad wanted peace between all the boys, particularly, but that it never happened. They were always at odds with each other or outwardly fighting. Mother was no help that day. She always took her eldest son Ralph's side, shouting all the while. Leigh and Nerida were in shock. Dad eventually got hold of the gun. It wasn't loaded. I brought the young boys back into the house, with Ralph attacking me verbally for taking them away.

'What were you thinking, Geb? [This has always been my nickname.] Nothing was ever going to happen!' shouted Ralph. 'It wasn't even loaded!'

For once, I shut my mouth. However, I did think, tell that to the many people killed by their families.

I don't think Ralph ever liked me. In fact, I am sure he didn't. After all, I had wasted the education he had paid for by becoming an actress. And I couldn't make my marriage work. Mother had told me he had said that. Marriage breakdowns are always the woman's fault, after all.

During this time, there had been a few boyfriends in and out the door, nothing really serious. Well, I had sometimes been serious, but, for them, I was merely a stepping stone to someone else. I have always said that I have never had a one-night stand; they just didn't call back.

Up until that point in my life, I had never felt like 'the one' in any man's life. I was always too scared of being abandoned so I allowed them too much rope. I was always too busy trying to show men how fabulous I am instead of simply allowing things to play out. Once, I had an ex say to me, 'It is not for you to tell me or show me how wonderful you are. That's for me to discover.'

Fair enough, but he went on. 'When two people enter a room, the man is with the woman or the woman is with the man. I am always with you and I hate it.'

I think he may have had a few issues.

Soon after *The Sentimental Bloke* I moved back to Sydney. It was 1976. I worked, for the only time, apart from a couple of concerts years later, at Marian Street Theatre, on the Upper North Shore of Sydney, in *Cole ... A Musical Tribute*, a musical revue about Cole Porter.

I did play there one Sunday matinee of *Side by Side by Sondheim* years later. I was having breakfast when I received a call saying that Judi Connelli was ill and that they were doing a matinee that day and they wondered if I would step in and do the matinee for her. I gulped and said 'yes' before I had a chance to think it through. I knew a lot of the songs. I was told I could hold a script and some music. Before I knew it, I was at Marian Street rehearsing for the late afternoon matinee. As the houselights went down, the announcement was made that Judi would not be appearing. There was a loud, negative reaction. I gulped again. Then the announcement that I was doing the show that day met with a huge round of applause. The audience was on side and very forgiving. It turned out to be one of those shows talked about for years, with people wishing they had been there.

In 1976, I returned home to Queensland Theatre Company to star in *A Toast to Melba*, having missed out on the role in Sydney at the Old Tote. They went with the opera singer, Jennifer McGregor, who played it to much success.

I loved playing Melba and it was great to return to my old stamping ground. Yes, I stayed at home, and yes, my mother continued to harass me and criticise my choices of just about anything, including clothing purchases. She couldn't help herself.

Later that year, I appeared in my first feature film, *Break Of Day*, directed by Ken Hannam and shot around beautiful Maldon, in Victoria. It wasn't a large role, but nevertheless, it was a good introduction into the world of film. I was part of a group of bohemians, the others including John Bell and

Dennis Olsen. The role was an interesting cameo. The following year, Ken offered me a terrific role in *Summerfield*, which we shot on Phillip Island in Victoria.

I am forever grateful to have been part of the huge resurgence of the Australian film industry during these years. It culminated in 1983, with my fabulous role of Vere in the classic, *Careful, He Might Hear You*. It was not until 2000 that I would appear in my next film, *The Wog Boy*, where I played, with relish, the wonderful role of Minister for Employment, Raelene Beagle-Thorpe. I played leading roles in more than a few TV movies over those years as well.

I returned to Sydney in 1976 and lived in Edgecliff for a time with my talented friend, Natalie Mosco, who had been in the original cast of *Hair* on Broadway and had appeared in many hit shows during her years living in Australia, including *Grease* and *The Magic Show*. She returned to New York the following year, but came back to Australia for a while and we appeared together in the premiere season in Australia of *Company* in the mid-eighties in Sydney.

When *The Wiz* had been on the road for a time and was playing in Sydney at Her Majesty's Theatre, J. C. Williamson's were having trouble with one of the witches. Betty Pounder asked me to learn the role secretly, so that, if there were another blow-up, they could replace her and I'd be ready to go. To this day, it is the weirdest job I have ever had. On several occasions, I had to arrive at the theatre for private coaching, almost in disguise, learn the solo, choreography and dialogue, and have secret costume fittings. Nothing came of it, but it was certainly interesting. This show, by the way, spelt the end for J. C. Williamson's theatres. It didn't help that many of the cast 'blacked up' for the show! Not good.

I took over for a time from Anne Semler, stalwart of the Music Hall in Neutral Bay, in *Lust For Power*, in 1977. The Music Hall was a very successful theatre restaurant in Neutral Bay in Sydney, one of a kind, presenting specially written shows, usually with colonial themes and original music, tailored for the venue. It operated from 1961 through 1980, when fire restrictions closed the doors. A few actors went from show to show there. These regulars told me of the time that one of the character actors threw his head back to laugh just before the show, fell back, had a heart attack and died. The dressing room was long and narrow. The cast thought the show would, naturally, be cancelled that night, but the management insisted they go on. There was a full house. So, after the understudy was ready, and until the ambulance arrived, they just had to keep stepping over the body to make their entrances.

Later that year, I was offered a leading role in *Ashes,* a play by David Rudkin, directed by Ken Horler at Nimrod Theatre. This was a big break for me into the legitimate theatre world in Sydney, playing opposite John Gaden, a well-known Sydney actor. I was so happy during this time, having always wanted to be considered an actor first. I was also mad about John.

The singularly most exciting thing to happen in 1977 was being a part of The International Music Theatre Forum, put together by Amy McGrath. It took place at Sydney Conservatorium of Music. Amy had convinced three giants of the American theatre, Stephen Sondheim, Harold Prince and Alan Jay Lerner to come to Sydney to take part. I still can't believe I met them when I was so young. I sang on the Australian musicals presentation day. I sang the lead in the musical of *The Harp in the South* by Peter Stannard and Alan Burke, and I played Lillie Langtry in the Ray Cook, David Mitchell, Melvyn Morrow piece, *That Mrs Langtry.*

I knew my performances went over well with the audience, but when I received a message backstage inviting me to supper at a north shore house, with Sondheim and Prince, I was beside myself. I walked into the room later that night to see Steve Sondheim holding a didgeridoo, which he had just bought after a backstage tour of the Sydney Opera House. He was really excited about the whole afternoon, the instrument, which he refused to put down the entire evening, and the opera house, which he praised generously. We sometimes forget just how thrilling it must be for overseas guests to see that magnificent building for the first time. I know whenever I work there, it is exciting every day as I make my approach.

This was the start of a long acquaintance with both of them. Hal wrote me many lovely notes over the years about various performances, as did Steve. Hal was always a great correspondent and supporter of mine. They were both great correspondents. I have kept all of their letters. I have appeared in more Sondheim shows, mostly premieres in Australia, than anyone, I believe. He, his music, and his shows have been a huge influence on my career.

When he was in Australia on 6 July 2007, I was chosen to sing during Steve's televised interview with Jonathan Biggins at the Theatre Royal in Sydney. This was to be the last time I saw Steve. While preparing in my dressing room, there was a knock at the door. It was Steve Sondheim. He said, 'Geraldine, I have a really heavy cold. I should be in bed recovering, but I don't want to let anyone down. I just want to let you to know if I get up and walk off stage while you're singing, it is to cough. I wouldn't want to disturb your performance.'

'Oh, okay,' I answered weakly.

I was in shock. Can you imagine starting to sing 'Could I Leave You' and Stephen Sondheim walking off stage? What would that signal to the live and television audience?

I was nervous as I was introduced and walked on to begin. It is confronting enough singing a great song a couple of metres away from the composer of that song.

Thankfully, Steve didn't walk off. He came to me afterwards and said, 'Geraldine. You were very, very good. You nailed it.' This is high praise from Sondheim. He was a little scary, but always fair.

Towards the end of that year, 1977, I auditioned for Reg Livermore for his and Patrick Flynn's new rock musical, *Ned Kelly*. I got the part of Mrs Kelly. We opened at the end of 1977 and played into 1978. This was a fine experience all round. We rehearsed and opened in Adelaide to poor reviews, undeserved. It was a wonderful cast. It was the first time I worked with the likes of Arthur Dignam, Colin Hay, Doug Parkinson and Jeremy Paul.

In rock musicals, in those days before microphone technology improved, you rehearsed microphone choreography, as you used hand-held microphones, with cords attached. So it was imperative to know at every second as you moved around the stage, where the cords ended up, so as not to have an embarrassment of 'spaghetti' on stage to unravel at the end of a sequence.

We also played Her Majesty's in Sydney, to better reviews, but that was where we closed. To this day, I believe it deserved a much, much longer run and much more praise, but that's showbiz. *Ned Kelly* is overdue for a revival.

In 1978, I was back at Nimrod, rehearsing and playing Dotty Moore in *Jumpers*, the Tom Stoppard play, a gift of a role, which had originally been played by Diana Rigg in London. Ken Horler directed. Ken had always been kind and generous to me. Neil Armfield, theatre and opera director, was assistant, one of his first jobs. John Gaden played opposite me. We remained friends, although our lives had taken different directions by then. The cast met and had a fabulous lunch with Tom Stoppard, when he visited Sydney to see the show.

The most memorable thing for me about this season was the fact that I had to be naked for twenty minutes in Act One. Anyone who has attended that theatre, now Belvoir, knows that patrons are quite close to the action, so all the more scary.

Luckily, at twenty-eight, I think I was at my peak physically. I had to appear to be really comfortable with being naked, as the nude scenes took place in my bedroom, while the character was having a nervous breakdown. To this day, I meet people, mostly men, who tell me they have never forgotten me in that play.

I managed to keep Mother away from this one. I put it in the 'too hard' basket.

It was during this season, I left my agency, June Cann Management and went over to Bill Shanahan and he became my best friend, confidante and manager. I was nervous about leaving June. She had been so good to me, and I felt a sense of disloyalty. I remember getting up early after a performance to front up and tell her. I walked in. Had a cup of tea. Chatted aimlessly. It was almost as if she picked up on something. I just couldn't bring myself to say anything. Suddenly, June announced that she wanted to redecorate the office.

'You have great taste, Geraldine. Why don't you take some measurements for new curtains? You and Hugh [her son who worked at the agency] go out and choose fabric. Buy some paint. I trust you implicitly.'

I said nothing. Smiled weakly.

So, I found myself up ladders, then out and about all day looking for fabric and paint colours. How could I tell her now? I told Hugh halfway through the afternoon. Rightly so, he said that I had to face it. I left that day having not faced it.

I got to the theatre early for the show. Called the agency. Told June over the phone why I had come in that day, almost vomiting as I spoke. She was gracious and forgiving. Such was the person she was.

This same year, 1978, I was asked to be part of a rather historic company, the Paris Company, a part of Sydney theatre history as it was short lived, but big with ambitions. The line-up from actors and directors to designers and producers was absolutely stellar, with actors like Judy Davis, Robyn Nevin, John Gaden, Kate Fitzpatrick, to designers like Brian Thomson, Oscar winner, Luciana Arrighi and Martin Sharp. The Paris Theatre was an old picture palace on the site of the now Connaught apartment building in Sydney at Whitlam Square. I was thrilled to be chosen to be a part of the actors' company, to be included with such luminaries, and with directors, Jim Sharman and Rex Cramphorn at the helm. This short-lived company had its own feel and flavour. We were to concentrate on new works. It was a pity it didn't last. However, as Alan Jay Lerner wrote:

Don't let it be forgot
That once there was a spot
For one brief shining moment ...

We did two shows, *Pandora's Cross,* a musical by Dorothy Hewett and Ralph Tyrrell and *Visions* by Louis Nowra. I was in the first, playing a stripper. I remember doing research in Kings Cross, seeing many strippers perform and talking to them about their lives. I had a number called 'I'll Striptease You', in which I stripped down to nothing, with huge feather boas hiding me until the last chord ... reveal, hands in the air, blackout!

The set was quite vertical, with several, individual playing areas. It was like acting on a bookshelf. I remember one night, Jennifer Claire doing a monologue before Arthur Dignam's monologue. We were all on stage in our separate areas. Jenny had a bit of trouble with her words that performance, but the audience wouldn't have known, until, that is, we got to the end of it and it was over to Arthur, who said, 'Now it's my turn, thank God, after she's forgotten so much of her speech and bored you all for so long.'

Talk about throwing someone under the bus!

Then he went on with his speech. We were all trying to keep it together. Naughty Arthur. I adored him.

I loved Jenny Claire as well. During rehearsals, she had not turned up to rehearsals for a couple of days. People had tried to call. She eventually turned up two days later to tell us that she had gone out drinking in The Cross, had picked someone up, had taken him back to her place, where he had tied her up and had sex with her. She had taken two days to escape. Those were the days!

In 1979, ABC television produced a series of jukebox musicals set in different eras, with music from those periods. There was a 1930s Hollywood one, a 1920s speakeasy one and a 1940s war years one, set on a troopship. The series was called TV Follies. I was in *Troopship*. I played, Doris La Salle, the star of the show. There was a running gag that every scene saw me slapping someone across the face. They were terrific productions. I spent a lot of the rest of that year doing gigs. I guested on TV shows, until, at the end of that year, I auditioned for *Evita*.

It opened the following year in Australia. I had seen the opening night on Broadway and had attended the fabulous opening night party at the Waldorf, with sumptuous ice sculptures and lashings of marvellous food. John Robertson, whom I had known since *No, No, Nanette* had taken me to this fantastic opening in New York. I really wanted that part. I didn't get it and the rest is history.

It remains one of two times in my career I have been bitterly disappointed about losing a role. I find there is no point getting upset over an audition. If you do your best and they go in a completely different direction, so be it. And I can honestly say that I have never begrudged anyone getting a job, even getting a part over me. In fact I wish them well.

This audition was special. The call-back women – there were four of us, Noni Hazelhurst, Michele Fawdon, Jennifer Murphy and I – had to bring costume changes, things we deemed appropriate for Eva, and we were there all day. Of course, Jennifer Murphy won the prized role. Good for her! It was a really thorough audition process. I actually enjoyed the day. Hal Prince knew me well, of course. Apparently as I walked on stage in my evening gown choice, he said, 'It's Phyllis from *Follies*.'

Strangely, that is a show I have never done.

The upshot of the whole day was that Hal walked down to the orchestra pit while I was on stage, having sung my lungs out, and told me I did not have the role. He said, 'Geraldine, what can I say? You are so talented. But you are too tall. Eva was short. Also, in the beginning of the show, when Eva enters, I want the audience to wonder if she will ever make it. Then, she becomes a star during the piece. You walk onto a stage and I know you're going to make it.'

I was thankful to hear straight away. Although flattered by his compliment about me, ever the actress, I left thinking that I could act the bit about looking as if I won't make it. I was incredibly disappointed and I vowed, as the eighties loomed and my career was about to burst, to never allow myself to be so invested in an audition again. There is always a fine balance to strike.

I didn't have to audition for my dream role in a musical in the early eighties. It was simply offered to me. Mother didn't care if I had to audition or not, as long as I got the show. All she ever wanted was to see me as a leading lady in the middle of the stage with my arms up.

8

I Know a Girl

It is early June 1981. We open on the 6th so we are doing a gypsy run a few days before – a dress rehearsal with an invited industry audience. This is a new production of the musical Chicago *for Sydney Theatre Company, directed by Richard Wherrett, choreographed by Ross Coleman, designed by Brian Thomson and with costumes by Roger Kirk. I am playing Velma Kelly, Nancye Hayes is Roxie. We have been working hard, as you do, but we don't really know how it will be received as it is a new concept, an original production. I know the choreography is brilliant and the ideas, with some cross-dressers as some of the female prisoners, and the amazing costumes and sets leave me breathless. Usually, Australia buys in a production of a big musical, so this is unusual, to have created our very own work and to be a part of that creation.*

The overture starts. We are all excited. It is a stellar cast. As the overture leads into 'All That Jazz' and I enter, the house explodes. At the end of the number, the audience goes wild, with a standing ovation. Time stands still. It actually stops the show. Applause rings out for minutes and we can't go on with the show until the explosion ends. It is thrilling. We know at that moment that we are a hit. What is to be an eight-week run at the Drama Theatre at the Sydney Opera House, turns into a two year and more, sold out, multi-award-winning season, playing the Theatre Royal in Sydney twice, with a season at Melbourne's Comedy Theatre, a tour of

Australia, then, a tour to Hong Kong the third year. I am a part of Australian theatre history and I cannot be more proud of us all.

❧

It was 1978, when Richard Wherrett was still one of the directors of Nimrod Theatre, that Pamela Gibbons and I pitched the idea of *Chicago* to Richard, to direct at Nimrod, with Pamela as Roxie and me as Velma. Pamela and I had remained close friends since *No, No, Nanette* and longed to do another show together. Richard liked the idea, but could not get the rights for a small theatre like Nimrod.

Unbeknown to us, Richard had applied to be the new artistic director of Sydney Theatre Company the following year and when he got the job, he reapplied for the rights.

I went to New York, my first trip to the US, in 1979. I stayed with Natalie Mosco in Tudor City, saw many shows, saw Hal Prince, who said he would help me all he could if I could get a work permit. I didn't. It was incredibly difficult in those days and even if you did, Equity might still not allow you to work on Broadway. I have only appeared in New York in cabaret as, of course, you are not taking someone else's job when you are being 'you'. That is allowed, with a special visa. These days, with the world opening up more, it is simpler to acquire a work permit and is a simpler process to acquire a Green Card.

I lapped up all the new experiences in New York, returned broke, a couple of months later, having let my rented flat go. Bill Shanahan asked me to move in with him and Kris Fredrikson. From the moment Bill and I met, it was love, absolute and never-ending. He was the brother I never had. I trusted him with my life. Bill and I had similar working-class backgrounds and there was an unspoken understanding between us about what it was like to have grown up with alcohol abuse, with a family you felt was totally foreign to you. Bill's mother had died when he was quite young. His father drank. It was a large Catholic family from Cundletown, in New South Wales.

I remember many stories Bill shared about growing up in a small town. The one that still makes me as sad is the story about him winning a bursary to go to a special school in a bigger town and how that would change his life. He said the town had a one-off church service, where the priest spoke highly of him and said that the whole town was proud of him. Bill sat in the church silently, as he knew he wasn't going to any special school. Nothing special was happening for him. His father had drunk all the money away. There was no bursary. Yet he sat there and took the praise from people, not wanting to embarrass his father. It broke my heart when he first told me. He told the story, with grace, and in a comedic way. But I knew exactly what he must have felt. I understood that sort of disappointment absolutely. I have been lucky in my life to make some really good friends, but Bill Shanahan … nothing has been like that. We were drawn to each other. He was not only my manager. He was my family. There was nothing I wouldn't do for him.

Bill had bought a house in Stanmore, in Sydney. Kris, Bill and I became very protective of one another, with many secrets shared. They were both gay. We set up a series of shorthand names to describe the passing parades of our male dates. A 'Mark' was the top of everything. If you met a 'Mark', well, goodness, you could only hope it would last. And it hardly ever did as a 'Mark' was someone you could only ever aspire to. Next down the ladder was a 'Steve', a very nice, perfectly acceptable, regular guy, but not a 'Mark'. And so on down. There were about five levels, the penultimate being a 'Bevan' … not so good, and then, if your date was just hideous, he was 'Beyond Bevan'. How we would laugh around the breakfast table when someone said they'd been out the night before and it was 'Beyond Bevan'!

I lived in Bill's house until 1983. I only moved out because it was too, too comfortable there and I couldn't see a way forward to a semblance of a normal life, with a partner perhaps, until I moved out on my own. I mean we were spoilt. We had Mitzi, our maid, who came every day, made our beds, cleaned up, prepared dinner if needed. It was the happiest time. So much laughter! I adored both Bill and Kris. Bill became my 'everything'. He was my best friend, manager, agent and protector. I didn't even have a handle on money. If I fell on hard times, he would simply top up my account. If times were great, he'd help me manage my funds. Honestly, I don't know what I'd have done without Bill. I depended on him so much. He was supposed to be there always.

I still don't know what to do without him, but I've had to learn.

I hold him responsible for my successful career. He was not only an agent, but also someone who constantly came up with ideas for my advancement. I knew I was on his mind and I knew what a lucky girl I was to have him in my life. I think about him every day. We lost him in the early nineties and I didn't know what hit me. A part of my heart was ripped out. It was unbearably hard, as hard as losing my mother.

I was asked to be in the first repertory company of the Sydney Theatre Company in 1980 and leapt at the opportunity. I am sure Bill had a hand in that. The first show we did was *The Sunny South* with a big cast, led by John Hargreaves, whom I adored. In fact, I fell in love with him, although he was gay. I'm sure he adored me as well, as he did ask me to marry him at one stage. His mother loved the notion of that. I thought the better of marrying someone who never had sex with me, but we remained adoring of each other and had a strangely intimate relationship for a time, then later became friends.

John was a wonderful actor and an extraordinary person, funny, charismatic, one of a kind. He once had all the flowers from a florist shop delivered to me, as he couldn't make up his mind which ones he preferred. We were as close as two people can be, without a sexual relationship, just like Bill and me. It was difficult to even consider walking away from someone who buys a whole florist shop for you. I adored that sort of mad generosity. And John's laugh, John's smile lit up the world. He would throw his head back and laugh and you felt totally embraced by him and adored.

He could be a bugger! Once, during *The Sunny South*, John and I went out and sat in the Bourbon and Beefsteak at Kings Cross all night, as you did in those days, with John drinking up a storm. Danny La Rue was there and John became a little entranced by him. So much so that as he hailed a cab for me in Taylor Square later, while people in business clothes waited for buses as the sun was well and truly up, he shouted, 'I hate cunts!'

I hopped in the cab and thought, I know that darling. So, now, does all of Darlinghurst!

John didn't turn up for work at the theatre that night. Stage management kept coming into my dressing room asking me where he was.

'How should I know?'

His agent couldn't raise him by phone, eventually going around to his house and banging on the door. He arrived, sheepish, at interval, by which time Andrew Tighe had gone on with a book and had done really well.

The next day, another florist shop was delivered to my house, with a note, 'Sorry, darling.'

Such was the repertory company in that first year of STC that one was cast in small roles, while the leads were brought in, although I had a lovely role in *The Sunny South*. I did not want small roles to be an ongoing reality for me. I remember trying to talk to Richard Wherrett about that. We had a conversation where he said, 'Geraldine, you are hardly an intellectual.' I was hurt by that comment.

A year later, Richard took that comment back, apologised for misjudging me. I loved him for that. We became friends and he gave me many wonderful opportunities over the years, more than any other director has.

Part of the first season was a show called, *I'm Getting My Act Together and Taking It on the Road*, which I had seen in New York and loved. Ross Coleman choreographed it. Nancye Hayes was brought in to play the lead and I had a great role with a terrific solo number. I guess Richard looked at Nancye and me working together, getting on so well, and thought again of *Chicago*.

We played Sydney and the Adelaide Festival to much success. Then, Bill and I had talks and negotiated with the STC to release me from the rest of my contract that year as I remained unhappy about doing virtually walk-on roles. Richard understood and released me to play larger roles that were being offered at Melbourne Theatre Company and beyond. It was hard to leave a full-time contract, but the rest of that year turned out to be fulfilling for me. It was the right choice. Anyway, I knew I had more work with STC the following year.

Richard had told me he had secured the rights of *Chicago* for 1981 and that he wanted Nancye and me for the leads. I was very excited but I was also worried about telling Pamela Gibbons. I felt disloyal and it did not sit well with me. Loyalty is something I hold dear. However, I was young and ambitious and this was a fabulous opportunity. To this day, I believe that, although we did not have a falling out, Pamela and I were never the same. Certainly, we have seen each other through the years, we have had talks, lunches, dinners, but we have never really put it to bed. As for me, I believe some decisions in life come with consequences that you have to own and continue to live with.

So, when I left STC in mid-1980, with the knowledge I was to do *Chicago* the following year, I appeared in the very first late night show at a Sydney theatre. It was Bill Shanahan's idea to do a cabaret show at weekends at Nimrod in the downstairs theatre. We called it *Geraldine Turner Sings*, not exactly an exceptional title, as we had themed passages about love, with music to match. But it worked well as it promoted my name.

We paid to have posters printed. Bill called me in to the office one day, just before the opening, and said he didn't know what we could do. The posters had been delivered and they were all wrong and there was no time to change them.

'Even your name is wrong.'

'What do you mean?' I said.

In fact, for a joke, Bill had done a mock-up poster, with the photo of a hundred-year-old woman, with warts all over her face and it read, 'Josephine Tupnup Sings'.

Floods of laughter all through the office! I still have that poster.

Max Lambert was the musical director and Tony Sheldon directed. It was a huge success. In fact, we eventually took the show to New York a few years later. Bill travelled with Max and me to New York. We had stayed in LA for a few days at Chateau Marmont and had the best time. We were all exhausted when we arrived in New York.

I remember we went to see a contemporary dance company perform at The Met. Then, having a huge shouting match with Bill after the show as we disagreed about the performance. We must have been tired as it was a ridiculous argument.

More ridiculous were the things that happened to darling Bill on a seemingly regular basis. After he had settled us into our New York run, Bill flew to London, where he had some business to do for other clients. He had decided that he would treat himself and stay in a huge suite at the very chic

Brown's Hotel. As he started to unpack his bathroom stuff, he opened the door of the bathroom cupboard to be confronted by a huge, fresh 'turd' sitting on the middle shelf. He called reception immediately and said, 'Would you mind sending someone up to my room? There is something in my bathroom cupboard.'

A rather pompous man in a morning suit arrived quite quickly and was in the bathroom for a very long time, presumably working out how to remove the offending item successfully. Bill waited for a flush. No flush. Finally the pompous man emerged, with a towel bundled up (I can only imagine it was evidence) and as he exited the room, he turned to Bill and said rather poshly, rolling those Rs, 'I'm terribly, terribly sorry, sir!'

Another story in the 'These things could only happen to Bill' catalogue took place back in Sydney. Bill was in a rush to go to see a screening of a film of one of his star clients.

At this point I must digress to say that the wonder of Bill Shanahan as an agent was that you understood there were much bigger stars at the agency, bigger money earners, but when he spoke to you, you believed you were his most important client. He never made anyone think they were less.

So, he was in a hurry, probably running late as he drove up Albion Street, a narrow, one-way, very hilly street near Central Station in Sydney. Cars were parked tightly on both sides of the steep hill. He looked around for a park. There was only one that he thought he could squeeze into, in front of a boat, a huge cruiser on wheels, parked on the left-hand side of the street. He managed the tight park and quickly rushed in to see the film.

After the screening, he had to rush back to the office. He pulled out and started driving up the narrow, hilly street, when he felt a pull, a sort of heaviness. He looked in the rear-view mirror and, to his shock, his car had somehow hooked on to the huge cruiser and he was towing it!

As he looked in his rear-view mirror, gasping in surprise, the cruiser dislodged and ran back down the hill. Now, it could have been disastrous, as the cruiser could have smashed into every car on both sides of the narrow street. Miraculously, the cruiser did not hit any car and slid straight back into the space from where it had come, smashing only into the gutter, doing some damage to the boat, but no cars.

Bill looked left. He looked right. No-one seemed to be around. He took off.

But there is always someone.

Later, back at the office, the local police called and asked Bill if he was aware that he had been in an accident on Albion Street a couple of hours earlier. A witness had taken his registration number.

'No, officer,' said Bill. 'I thought my car was rather sluggish as I pulled out and drove up the hill, but it seemed to right itself.'

'You're telling me you had no idea you were towing a huge cruiser, sir?'

'Sorry, officer. Apart from my sluggish car, which I did think odd, no.'

In 1980, I played Mrs Kendall, a great part, in *The Elephant Man* for Melbourne Theatre Company. I adored this play. I had seen it on Broadway, so when it was offered, I rushed at the opportunity. I have realised over time that I am always happiest when I am part of a company and being considered a 'legitimate actor'. This is ridiculous really, as starring in a musical takes many more skills and disciplines. But some folk who love theatre hate musical theatre and do think of it as a lesser theatrical form. Sometimes, you are treated as if you are not quite an actor, when starring in a musical.

I think it is because musicals are easy to do badly. The only difference in 'acting' in musicals is when the character starts to sing. It is because the emotion doesn't allow the character to simply speak. The song that follows is heightened reality but still based in truth, or it doesn't work. I have, at times, worked with very good actors, who are cast in a musical and all reality goes out the window. Suddenly, instead of an authentic performance, they start mugging and playing out front. No wonder musicals are thought of as second rate, in some circles! This sort of performance gives them a bad name.

After the very successful season of *The Elephant Man*, I was approached by Graeme Murphy, Artistic Director of Sydney Dance Company, to not only appear in a new ballet with the company, but to put together the music and storyline of a ballet called *An Evening*, with Graeme, Janet Vernon, and Max Lambert.

This was an exhilarating time of creativity, with much arguing; well … banter, and fun and much work. I did class every morning with the company.

Max and I flew to Hobart to rehearse the string quartet we had hired. The result was wonderful. Our part of the ballet was arranged for string quartet and piano. To watch the dancers emerge from 'frightened to sing', to 'loving singing' was a wonderful thing. And I danced with them. I sang a lot as well, of course. I performed a *pas de trois* with Graeme and Janet. We toured. It was very successful. Years later, Janet and I performed our very beautiful song, dance sequence as part of a tribute to Graeme at a special gala celebrating his career. I hold the entire experience and those dancers very dear to me. I went on to begin rehearsals for *Chicago* and Jill Perryman took over my part in *An Evening* for the rest of the tour.

Chicago ... our production is still talked about as a benchmark. We were lauded. We sold standing room every night. We were a very happy company. We recorded a cast album, which I am very proud of. It sold well at the time. It is now a collector's item.

Apart from the innovative set and costumes and Richard's fantastic direction, Ross Coleman's choreography was utterly brilliant. Ross was a genius, in that Fosse way. He could be a monster. I recall walking out of a rehearsal, when Ross was setting 'Cell Block Tango' as he was treating a couple of the women in the cast in an abominable way. I refused to return to the room until he apologised to them. But how I loved him. Ross choreographed many, many of my shows and he knew how to make me look good. We were close friends. When his mother died, he asked me to sing at the funeral, but I said that, as I had known Dulcie very well, it would be too upsetting for me.

He asked Rhonda Burchmore, who flew up from Melbourne for the funeral. As she began to sing a jazz version of 'Life Is Just a Bowl of Cherries', in the middle of the service, Ross suddenly stood up and started to dance around the coffin in an improvised routine. It was strange. It was extraordinary. It was funny. It was sad. It was confronting. Many of his dancers, those he had continued to cast over the years, were there and found the whole 'interpretive dance around the coffin' very moving. I did ask Rhonda afterwards if she knew this was going to happen. From the look on her face, I knew she didn't.

LEFT: Little me, in Mum's tulip-pocket dress, 1953.

BELOW: With my brother, Leigh … Mother made the hat as well, 1954.

ABOVE LEFT: Holding a koala at Lone Pine Sanctuary, 1955.

ABOVE RIGHT: Handing out free cigarettes to the ladies, at Her Majesty's Theatre Brisbane in 1959, during *Oriental Cavalcade*.

LEFT: With Mum and Dad, 1958.

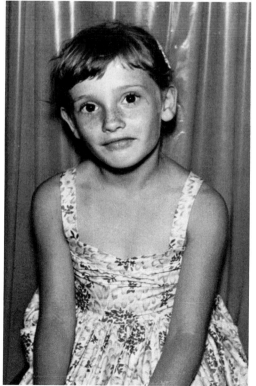

ABOVE: The Turners at my brother Ray's wedding in 1967. From left to right, Noel, Ralph, Ray, Val, the bride, Leigh, Mum, Geraldine and Dad.

LEFT: Looking straight at the camera with big, wide eyes in 1960.

ABOVE LEFT: As Betty from Boston in *No, No Nanette*, with Paul Wallace, 1972, for Williamson-Edgley Theatres. From my private collection.

ABOVE RIGHT: As Petra in *A Little Night Music*, with Tim Page, 1973–74, J. C. Williamson productions. From my private collection.

LEFT: As Velma in *Chicago*, for Sydney Theatre Company, 1981–82. (PHOTO: BRETT HILDER)

ABOVE LEFT: As Nancy in *Oliver*, 1983–84, Adelaide Festival Trust. From my private collection.

ABOVE RIGHT: As Joanne in *Company*, 1986, for Sydney Theatre Company. (PHOTO: DON MCMURDO)

RIGHT: As Mrs Lovett in *Sweeney Todd*, 1987–88, for Melbourne Theatre Company.

ABOVE: As Reno Sweeney in *Anything Goes*, with my Angels, for Hayden Attractions Pty Ltd/Victoria State Opera/Bill Armstrong, 1989–91. (PHOTO: BRANCO GAICA)

LEFT: With Bill Shanahan, at my 40th birthday party in 1990. From my private collection.

RIGHT: As Desirée in *A Little Night Music*, 1991, for Sydney Theatre Company. (PHOTO: HUGH HAMILTON)

BELOW: As the Baker's Wife in *Into the Woods*, 1992, for Sydney Theatre Company. (PHOTO: ROBERT MCFARLANE)

ABOVE: Performing in *Cabaret* in Sydney, 1996. From my private collection.

BELOW LEFT: Performing in *Cabaret* in Berlin, 1999. From my private collection.

BELOW RIGHT: With Brian – the diva and the maestro. From my private collection.
(PHOTO: STUART CAMPBELL)

We lost Ross suddenly in 2009. The first person I called was Nancye. We had all been through so much together. I was touring with *Steel Magnolias* at the time. I was grateful that Jacki Weaver and I could be in attendance at Ross's burial, while on our way to another venue for the play in regional Victoria. Ross was a friend, a searing talent, infuriating and altogether wonderful. I feel like he was my official choreographer as I worked with him so much over the years. He was such a presence in my life. I still think I'll run into Ross sometimes.

The season of *Chicago* at the Drama Theatre extended, then moved to the Theatre Royal in Sydney, followed by more seasons there – all sold out. We played five shows each weekend: back-to-back shows on Fridays, a regular matinee and evening show on Saturdays and a Sunday afternoon show. I have never felt so tired. Walking up that long flight of stairs to stage door each Sunday, with every joint and muscle hurting was extremely challenging.

I recall, during the first Sydney season at the Theatre Royal, really taking a liking to one of the trumpet players who came in every now and again to play. He used to smile at me, or so I thought. He was a potential 'Mark'! Or so I thought.

I talked to my dresser about it, as you do, and she suggested I ask him to go to supper. Why wouldn't he want to go out with one of the leading ladies? I was too scared, so next time he was in, I asked her to do it for me. She chatted to him, God love her, and eventually said to him that Geraldine Turner would like him to join her for supper. He said, 'Which one is she?'

Last time I ever did anything like that. Beyond Bevan!!!

So, things went smoothly with the show as the whole cast bathed in our success. Then we arrived in Melbourne for the season at the Comedy Theatre. My heart sank when I saw the billboard outside the theatre and the program. My billing was incorrect. Nancye and I were contracted for our names to be on the same line, side by side, with her name first, as it should be, with Terry Donovan, a wonderful Billy Flynn on the second line in the centre. Instead, there it was: Nancye on the first line, mine underneath on the second line and Terry underneath on the third line. It appeared in the same way in the program, which of course they refused to reprint. I was furious. This was my first big, commercial leading role and this was important to me.

The management sent me a huge bunch of flowers, which I binned. Then, Richard Wherrett came in to my dressing room to reason with me as I was threatening to walk out. As if I ever would.

I remember getting so angry that I screamed at him to get out of my dressing room, as I threw a shoe at him, just missing his head. This incident is documented in his book and at my fortieth birthday at Bill's house some years later, Richard made a speech and talked of the shoe-throwing incident in a very amusing and loving way.

Eventually, Bill came to the rescue, egged on by Richard, and spoke to me on the phone, told me how sorry everyone was for the error, but that nothing could be done. I just had to agree to suck it up, as you seem to do so much during a career, and so we pushed on.

During the last Sydney season, we realised we had been playing eight shows a week for two years. Neither Nancye nor I had missed a performance. There weren't too many weeks left of the season. I had been flying back and forth from Melbourne recording a television panel show called *Beauty and the Beast* on a regular basis and I was running on empty, exhausted, doing both jobs and trying to keep everything going and my energy up.

This particular night, at interval, Max Lambert, who was playing keyboard that night, was in my dressing room chatting away, when I suddenly announced I couldn't hear him. He said, 'Don't be stupid. Of course you can hear me.' I did hear him say that, but it all felt a little disconcerting. I thought I was going mad.

I went on for Act Two. I was fine, but nervous and rather twitchy. We got to the scene before 'When Velma Takes the Stand', a scene with Billy Flynn. Terry Donovan started talking and I couldn't hear him. I kept watching his mouth and when it stopped I said my next line. Buzzing started in my head. I was completely panicked and parched. I think I shouted my lines, as I couldn't hear myself either. I was having a full panic attack on stage in front of a full house.

My number started. I managed the song, but as the dance routine started with my boys, everything appeared to go into slow motion in my mind and my feet and legs felt like they were going through the stage floor with each dance step, as if it were an ocean and not a hard surface. Everything was swaying as well. It's a wonder I didn't pass out.

Of course, we got through it somehow ... Doctor Footlights!

I exited and passed out in the wings. The boys carried me to my dressing room. I woke up, kept on saying, through floods of tears, that I could finish the show. Our company manager made the decision that I could go on as I kept assuring him that I could. So I got through it. Our company manager gave me four Valium and sent me home in a cab. I took them all and was awake all night. That's how wound up I was.

This is the same company manager who, every now and then, would go to each dressing room and warn everyone that his younger sister might appear in the wings that particular night. This happened on a semi-regular basis. If you happened to glance into the wings on those nights, while on stage, you would glimpse our company manager, Johnny Whitham, in full drag, in an outrageous wig, a beaded dress, full makeup, false eyelashes and stiletto heels strutting about in the wings, or simply standing there watching the action on stage. That kind of outrageous fun has well gone from the theatre nowadays, sadly.

Johnny was an impeccable dresser, perfectly turned out. He wore fabulous jewellery. He used to get all his clothes sent out to a well-known department store to be laundered, dry cleaned and pressed each week. His shirts would be delivered to the theatre, starched and pressed, in beautiful boxes. What a fantastic character he was.

After my panic attack, the management made me see a psychiatrist the next day and take that day off. The doctor said I needed a complete rest, as if that were possible. So he put me on a course of drugs to get me through the rest of the season. I was completely fine when I was able to slow down, get some rest and not feel as if I had to perform constantly. I did have one more panic attack at the hairdressers a week later. As I lay back to have my hair washed at the basin, I suddenly felt that panic rush. I remember running out of the salon, with wet hair and suds all over me, scaring people in the streets of Woollahra in Sydney.

As a postscript to that incident, the next day when I saw the psychiatrist was a matinee day. I was very pleased for my understudy, Pamela French, who got to play Velma twice, but that was the day Peter Allen came to see the show and I missed it. I did, however, work with Peter at the opening concert of the Sydney Entertainment Centre, where he wore that famous Australian flag shirt and sang 'I Still Call Australia Home' before it was such a well-known anthem.

A few weeks later, the final *Chicago* arrived. We didn't know at the time that we would play Hong Kong a year later. What a journey it had been. I could hardly sing 'Nowadays' for the tears. Nancye was the same. We were awash.

A year later, we all came together to start rehearsals for the Hong Kong season. There were some replacements in the company by then. Richard Wherrett could be a very funny person. He said, 'Okay. Let's do a run! Go!'

We did a sort of run, some of us remembering it all, clever us. It was impossible for the new cast, who didn't know any of it. They stumbled through, laughing. It turned out to be a wonderful bonding exercise as we chortled our way through an altogether wonderful day. What a wonder Richard was.

Our Hong Kong tour was exciting. Both Sue Nattrass and Christine Dunstan were on board by then. We performed at the Hong Kong Arts Festival at an old theatre, a barn of a place, on the island. The set had been built in Hong Kong. I think there had been somewhat of a language problem as there were many mistakes made, much to the despair of Brian Thomson, the designer, and the technical staff. Eventually, it was sorted. We coped with the differences and pushed on. We performed for a few weeks, and our audiences were good, although the reaction, the laughs, were not as forthcoming.

What I remember mostly is the frantic purchases we all made. Shops were open well into the night. I thought I'd died and gone to heaven as I could go shopping after the show. Someone in the cast would arrive at the theatre in a new outfit, with new shoes, and we would interrogate that person about where he or she had bought the item of clothing and the bargain price of said item. By the next day, we all had that shirt or dress or trousers. I think I spent most of my earnings from Hong Kong on new clothes.

With this show and tour, my mother got to see my name in lights at last. And I was in the middle with my arms up. I was happy about that, happy for her. I remember, as if it were yesterday, one of her visits to see the show in Melbourne. There were many, of course. She never said I was good. It was not until she died that I found out from many people how proud she was of me.

This particular time, I flew her down to see me. I was staying in an apartment a couple of blocks from the theatre. Mum wanted to do some washing one day, as I headed off to a matinee. I said I could send it to a laundry, as the washing machine in the apartment was not working.

'Mum. It's not working. Don't use the washing machine!' I remember being emphatic.

I came back between shows to find Mother on her hands and knees, trying to clean water that had flooded out of the machine, with soap suds gushing onto the carpet in the living room. I lost it and yelled at her. I was vicious as I accused her of never listening to me, never taking me seriously, always criticising, always trying to control me. It all poured out of me as if all those years of her dramas had led to this moment.

'I told you, Mum. I made it very clear. Don't use the washing machine! For Christ's sake, why did you do it?' I screamed.

This was all I needed when I just wanted to have a break, a rest and dinner between shows.

When we finished cleaning the mess, Mum was calm. She was quiet. She looked sad. She didn't scream at me. She didn't insult me. She no longer argued. She became very quiet and simply came in for the kill.

'One day I'll be dead and you'll remember this day and how you spoke to your mother.'

9

If Love Were All

*I*t is the end of September 1982. My mother is dead. What do I do it for now? All I've ever wanted is her approval. How do I perform just for me? Is that a good enough reason? Do I need a reason?

I know I have talent. My whole life up to this point has been about performing. Who am I if I am not performing? This is what I do. This is who I am. However it is years before I work it all out. There is a huge hole in me that I have never filled. I have never felt loved. I have never felt a part of my family. I do feel part of my housemates' family and certainly part of my wider theatrical family. That is why I am bereft when a show closes and I feel that all-too-familiar sinking flatness that all performers feel. Will I ever get another job?

I come to the conclusion that I just have to keep going, one foot in front of the other, and things will become clear. If they do not, well, I'll keep going anyway. I must find a way to fill that hole inside.

୬

When *Chicago* closed in Sydney in 1982, before my mother died, before my breast reduction surgery, I was asked to do a cabaret show at the old Motor Club in Sydney, which had been renamed 'The Upstage', a rather unfortunate name. Ken and Lillian Horler, whom I had known since Nimrod days, were opening this new venue as a theatre restaurant and wanted a gritty, political revue, a two-hander with John O'May and me, and Michael Tyack and Max Lambert on duelling pianos.

We arrived for the first day of rehearsals to find that there was no script. We spent most of the rehearsal period writing one, although we didn't have experience with gritty, political satire. So the show became more of a musical theatre, American popular song kind of show, with bits of satire interspersed. It bombed, big time.

It was a vast room. It sat hundreds and hundreds and the room had a huge post in the middle of the front of the stage. I'm sure this post or column held up the building. It was unfortunate, to say the least. It meant that, wherever you stood on stage, there were several people in the audience who couldn't see you, so much so that we made references to it, as part of the script.

We used to arrive each night and ask how many people had booked. 'Ten', Lillian would say, as our hearts sank.

'Fifteen tonight,' she would smile.

I think at weekends we sometimes played to twenty or twenty-five!

Usually, when you are literally 'dying' out on stage, with empty houses and not much hope of a turnaround, you tend to get your notice quite soon after opening and close not long after. But for some unknown reason, we went on and on for around sixteen weeks, crawling towards a closing night. I guess Ken and Lillian thought their fortunes might suddenly change for the better.

What a surprise it was then that one Friday night, we arrived to a full house, a noisy, chatty, happy lot who were all wearing party hats and had hooters. Never a good sign.

They were a convention. They had been convening and drinking since around four that afternoon. They were eating dinner and continuing to drink. Tetsuya Wakuda, who was to become a very famous Australian chef, was in charge of the kitchen so the food was fabulous. He fed us each night.

We went on for Act One at nine. We started the show. The audience was very drunk. They talked loudly throughout, shouted at us at times, threw food at us and blew their hooters regularly. It was difficult to concentrate let alone avoid stepping in prawns on the stage. The whole thing was humiliating.

We got through Act One and fled to the dressing room, which we all shared. We all started ranting as only actors can. The collective noun for actors is a 'whinge' of actors.

'Well, if they think we're going on for Act Two, they've got another thing coming!'

'I have never been so humiliated in my life!'

'I smell of old prawns!'

'Get Ken Horler back here. If he thinks we're going on for the second half, well he can whistle Dixie!'

'Yes. Get Ken back here. We shouldn't have to put up with this sort of treatment! We refuse to go back out there!'

Just as we were all ranting, talking over the top of one another, Ken walked into the dressing room and said, 'They don't want Act Two. They hate you!'

We immediately launched into, 'What do you mean? We want to do Act Two!'

A whinge of actors!

We closed, eventually. Then I went into hospital for my breast reduction surgery. My thoughts rushed back to dear old Freddie Carpenter saying, 'I'd spare no expense!' Well, Freddie, I hadn't done too badly up till then.

Mum had planned to come down to the Stanmore house to look after me after my hospital stay. The last time she had visited, earlier that year after *Chicago* closed, I remember her bursting into tears one night, seemingly for no reason, as Bill and I prepared dinner, joking and sharing stories.

'What's up?' I said. I wondered what she was thinking about. To this day, I wonder. All she said was, 'Nothing. I'm just happy.'

I was just out of hospital when the police came to the door on that fateful Sunday in September 1982, when everything changed for me. Dad couldn't remember my number. He was in shock. As Mum had died at my brother Ralph's house while they were visiting, Dad remembered I lived in Stanmore with Bill Shanahan, hence the police at the door and that awful shock.

I went to my surgeon to get my stitches out on the way to the airport, where I met my brother Leigh, who had flown in from Perth, and we flew up to Brisbane together for the funeral.

Dad actually sent me a letter a few weeks later. In it, he told me he loved Mum, had always loved her. I still have the letter. I'm glad I have it. I'm glad he wrote it.

But I remember sadness, uneasiness, fear, violence, but never any sort of love. Was this the time for me to write back to him, to confront him about the way he treated Mum, about growing up with all that violence, about what that does to a little girl, about the gaping hole inside me? I thought the better of it. I never had that conversation with my father. All I knew was that no happiness had ever come from our family.

I had appeared in a Bob Hope tribute on television, with Bob Hope himself joining us in the finale, and 1983 was full of similar one-off jobs and concerts. I also appeared in a tribute to Jerry Herman on *The Midday Show* a couple of years later, with Jerry accompanying us on piano; all too wonderful.

I appeared in the film, *Careful He Might Hear You* in 1983, an altogether wonderful experience and a fantastic cast. Interesting then, that mid-year, John Hargreaves, Wendy Hughes, Robyn Nevin and I appeared together again in *Present Laughter*, the wonderful Noel Coward play, for Sydney Theatre Company. We played the Theatre Royal in Sydney for a number of weeks. It was produced as a commercial season. This was unusual for Sydney Theatre Company. Directed by Richard Wherrett, it was a marvellous production, looked exceptional and John was a wonder in the central role, surrounded by the three of us, who were fabulous as the women in his life. It opened on my mother's birthday, 4 June.

At the end of 1983, I was offered Nancy in *Oliver!* for the Adelaide Festival Trust, opposite the wonderful Garry McDonald, who was a sensational Fagin. We rehearsed and opened in Adelaide on 7 January 1984.

I used to walk down from North Adelaide where I was staying, to the Festival Centre rehearsal rooms. One day, on my way to rehearsals, I was crossing the river, when a man came up from under the bridge and grabbed me from behind. I was in shock, but I surprised myself with my response. In hindsight it was stupid, as he could have been armed. I shouted at him. 'How dare you' Don't touch me! Let go of me! Get your hands off me!'

I wrestled him as well. I started hitting him. Every bone in my body rushed back to that night, when I was just seventeen and had been raped after winning *New Faces*. This time, I was not going to let anything happen to me without a fight! I didn't think of the consequences. I fought ... and fought. He did eventually let go and he ran away.

I got to rehearsal and fell apart. By then I was a blubbering mess after what I'd been through and was sent home for the day.

Just before I flew to Adelaide to start rehearsals for this most prized of roles, I met Greg Jones, who was to become my partner for almost a decade. At the time, Greg worked for Frank Walker, a minister in the Wran Government in New South Wales. He had also been a partner in a set-building company in Sydney and had a good knowledge of the theatre. A few years down the track, he became a producer.

I thought I had met the man I would be with for the rest of my life. Certainly, when my dad flew down for the opening night of *Oliver!* in Melbourne at my favourite theatre, Her Majesty's, he said that he was happy that at last I seemed settled, that he felt he could stop worrying about me. It was nice to hear he did worry about me.

I believe, to this day, that Nancy is one of the best things I've ever done, along with my Mrs Lovett in *Sweeney Todd*. I possess the qualities needed to play Nancy. She is vulnerable. She can be loud and raucous. She is also kind and loving. She is playful and caring with the children. In other words, there are layers to the character. Up until then, I had always played brash roles like Velma in musicals, apart from my short stint in Sydney a few years before, playing Sarah in *Guys and Dolls* at South Sydney Junior's Leagues Club, where the director, after our first very ordinary read through, famously said, 'Well that's great, just great. It just needs a little bit of polishing before the opening.'

The little bit of polishing included getting used to nudes in the show. In every production at South's in those days, it was mandatory to include topless girls in at least one scene. I was playing Sarah, the Salvation Army girl, the very staid girl, the very conservative girl, who is romanced by Skye Masterton and whipped away to a nightclub south of the border. Every performance, I had to pretend I didn't see eight nudes, who were right in front of my eyes in the club as I entered.

In *Oliver!*, Nancy's big voice must soar in Act Two, when she sings the heartfelt 'As Long As He Needs Me'. The role is a gift. This was the third professional production of this original version of the show in Australia and I loved carrying the knowledge of that history along with me every night. The first Nancy had been Sheila Bradley. The second had been Toni Lamond. Some years later at one of the first Helpmann Awards, when Tamsin Carroll was about to play Nancy in Cameron Macintosh's new version, all of the Australian women who'd played the role appeared together. Sheila Bradley, Toni Lamond, Lola Nixon, Tamsin Carroll and I each sang a solo section of 'As Long As He Needs Me' and then we all sang together from the key change. It was one of those thrilling moments in the theatre and so great to be a part of.

We played *Oliver!* in Adelaide and Melbourne only. We didn't do well enough in Melbourne to warrant a Sydney transfer. Garry didn't get great reviews, although he was a wonderful Fagin. They said he played it for laughs. Newsflash! It is a comedy role! The casting of the boys in Melbourne had a lot to do with us not doing too well. The Dodgers were great. It was the Olivers who were underwhelming in Melbourne. I guess we had been spoilt in Adelaide with two absolutely wonderful leading boys. One of the boys in Melbourne was fine, the other had no charm whatsoever and an Oliver can get away with an ordinary voice but the boy must possess loads of charm. That is a prerequisite.

Garry named this charmless boy, Rover. Cast members could be heard at stage door, signing on some nights and saying, 'Oh is Rover on? Bugger! I've got friends in.'

I was gutted about not transferring to Sydney. I do believe that original production, which we did, with 'the revolve' as part of the set, is far superior to the later version. For starters, it sets up an entrance round of applause for Nancy, which the new production does not allow. That is not the only reason, of course. I love the old London feel of that original set and 'the revolve' keeps the show flowing, which helps the storytelling.

Towards the end of our Adelaide season, I found I was pregnant. Those few weeks were the happiest I can remember in my life to that point. But a few weeks later, I miscarried. Greg was visiting and we were walking around

Adelaide zoo. I said I felt dreadful and that I thought I was miscarrying, but Greg made me keep walking. Why? And why did I agree?

After an ultrasound later that week, which showed there was no longer a baby, as I had suspected, I made an appointment for the minor surgery needed after a miscarriage for the week after the opening in Melbourne. No-one knew, apart from our company manager and stage manager. I never missed a show, not even on the day of my surgery.

I was hurt at the time that Greg didn't seem too upset and didn't want to talk about it. There were already chinks in the relationship so early into it, but I dismissed them. After all, my father approved of him so I must fight for this relationship. Greg was already presenting everything, no matter how things really were, on an upbeat, positive note. He was prone to exaggerating the truth. I have never been a fan of that at all.

The visit from my father to the opening night of *Oliver!* in Melbourne was to be the last time I ever saw him. I never told him about the pregnancy. My last image of him was very early one morning, leaving for the airport by taxi, which we had booked the night before. I had offered to take him, but he said I should sleep in, as it was a two-show day. I opened my eyes to watch him tiptoeing around the kitchen, making tea and toast and then leaving quietly so as not to wake me, carrying his suitcase, looking like a shadow of the man he had been in my youth.

Although I didn't ever have that long talk with my father about growing up with all that violence, I also didn't feel a sense that things were unresolved between us. I can't say why. I was lucky to have had two years with him after Mum died. She was such an influence, such a massive presence in my life, that when I called home on a regular basis, I tended to speak to her. Dad was always in the background. So those two years were for him and me. He was the star of my phone calls. We laughed together. We spoke of Mum. We spoke of my career and how proud he was of me.

There was nothing I needed to say to him. There was nothing to resolve. I do wish that all of the boys had got on with each other. That would have been a lovely thing for him, all he ever wanted. But it was never to be.

10

Sometimes I'm Happy

Oliver! *is finished. Greg and I move to a bigger, more glamorous apartment in the city in Sydney. I am asked to do a show at a new venue, Rose's, a cabaret room with host, Rose Jackson, a well-known drag queen. It is a show put together for the both of us, called* Sweethearts on Parade, *named after an Elton John song I had recorded. I am feeling quite unwell during rehearsals. I think I am pregnant again, but I don't tell Greg, as I am unsure. I have to lie down a lot during choreography rehearsals as I am in much pain. Still, I push on, hoping things will settle down.*

Late one night, we are asleep, when the phone rings and startles us. I answer. It is my brother Ralph. I never hear from him unless it is bad news.

He tells me Dad has died.

Dad has moved up to the Sunshine Coast to live with Ralph and his family at their urging. After only a month or so, there is a big blow-up, a huge falling out, unsurprisingly, and Dad moves out into a small flat he can afford to rent on his pension. I think he is fairly happy as he starts art classes, something he has always wanted to do. I still have a few of his paintings. But I remain disappointed that Ralph has uprooted Dad from his life and friends in Brisbane to seemingly dump him.

The thing is, he is not well. I have no idea, as I am not told. Dad goes into hospital with chest pains. Ralph doesn't even let me know Dad is in hospital. My family is the end, honestly. It is all too late now. I hang up after the awkward talk with Ralph.

I turn to Greg and tell him that Dad is dead. I am grabbing for my dressing gown to walk into the kitchen to put the kettle on, Mum's cure for everything.

As I am visibly upset, obviously needing support and comfort from my partner, starting to cry as I slowly move to the kitchen, Greg says, 'Do you want me to get up?'

My father's funeral was hard. Ralph had a crate of beer in the boot of his car at the burial ground. I found that shocking. He kept drinking throughout the service; not a good look! Dad was laid to rest next to Mum. Noel said, 'I'll be next.'

He was right. Dad died almost two years to the day after Mum. Noel died exactly two years later. His life had swung out of control the last few years. Noel had moved in with a woman in Kingaroy in Queensland. He seemed to be scared of her. He called me and asked for some money so he could escape her while she was at work and move back to Brisbane. Of course, I sent it.

Ralph called to tell me that Noel had died. I knew something was up as the family's grim reaper only ever called with bad news. After I answered the phone Ralph said, 'Noel. Dead.'

Well … not even, 'Hello. It's Ralph.'

Apparently Noel had been on his way to Sydney on the train. I think he was coming to see me to give me back the money I had sent him. He was drinking heavily, being loud and disturbing the passengers. The conductor put him off the train at Kyogle. It was only a few days later the police broke into his place in Brisbane to find the house full of empty bottles and Noel, dead.

He had drunk himself to death, had a heart attack. I think of him often; his sad life, which held such promise. Yes, his life, his incredibly bad choices, that split-second decision to punch little Michelle and the consequences that followed, the violence, the anger, his incapability to try to pick himself up and start again were all his doing, but even so, it was unbearably sad. I think he may have had a different life if he had followed his dreams and become a graphic designer, or had invented comic book characters, like he did when he was a teen. Instead, Noel took a very different, dark path. How could it have ended up with killing a young child in a violent rage, with years of prison, with years of pain about what he had become? I don't know why Noel drank so much. I don't know why drunken violence was ever present in our family. I don't know why good people can turn into someone they never imagined. Is it simply that they are angry about their lack of choices in life and their inability to choose a real way out, so violence becomes a way of venting, until the next crisis? Does the alcohol work in dulling all the pain and supplying a false confidence for a few hours? I think not. It is like any drug. You need more and more simply to feel a sense of normal.

What I do know is I am left with a deep unhappiness about Noel, so deep that it is a part of me that will never go away. When I think of him, I remember a kind brother when I was growing up. I remember someone who was always genuinely interested in what I was doing, in what I had to say. There were some good times, some laughter. But the sadness is always seeping through me.

Noel was buried next to Mum and Dad. It was fitting. He'd like that.

I didn't ever open in the show at Rose's as my pregnancy turned out to be ectopic. Fabulous Gaye McFarlane stepped into the show and learnt it within days of the opening. I was rushed into surgery, had my right tube removed.

Greg turned up at the hospital with a beautiful string of pearls with a ruby and diamond clasp. Gorgeous, but I would rather he had talked to me. He did take me on a holiday to the Gold Coast to help with my recovery, along with Patti Mostyn, legendary publicist and her husband, Eric Robinson, the owner of a famed sound design company. We rented a huge penthouse at Currumbin Beach with a big, big terrace, with private, separate areas for both couples. It was a lovely place, a lovely break, but Greg and I never really spoke of the loss. I needed to. We didn't ever connect about the important things. The loss of those two babies with Greg was to be an ongoing sadness for me, particularly as I never got pregnant again. He was not someone who wished to confront anything difficult. Better to be the positive, fun, upbeat kind of guy.

Patti and Eric had been regular guests at our house for lunches, dinners, and parties. During one dinner in particular, much drinking had taken place and had obviously continued when they had arrived home. The phone rang in the middle of the night, with Patti screaming down the phone, accusing me of stealing one of her special diamond earrings that Elton John had given her. She had been home for a few hours, and had noticed it was missing as she was cleaning up and fussing, and I presume drinking, in her kitchen.

After I told her I have never stolen anything in my life, I asked her to be reasonable and to think about it logically. 'Patti, why would I take one earring? And just how would I get it out of your ear without you noticing?'

'I don't know, but it's gone. You were the last person I saw so it must have been you!' She kept ranting.

After much cajoling, she started to calm down. She accepted that something else must have happened. We finished the call and I tried to go back to sleep, although I was more than a little cross by then and found it difficult.

The next morning, late, Patti called to say she was putting the kitchen bin out and noticed something sparkling at the top of the bin bag. There was her earring, stuck to a piece of old, browning avocado. Just recently, Patti and I talked and laughed about the incident.

I have to say, Greg was and still is an extremely amusing person. I think we stayed together so many years because we often laughed, really laughed. I adore people who can make me laugh. Always have. We were great hosts as well. Many a fabulous lunch turned into dinner and late night musings as we wended our way through the eighties. Producer, Helen Montagu brought Lionel Bart to lunch one day, for instance. Somewhere a photo exists of Lionel swimming in our pool. I talked to him of my time in *Oliver!* and how much I loved being in his wonderful musical.

The years flew by. It remained a great sadness that I never had a child, but time passing made things seem easier and there are many young people I continue to mentor.

My recording career began in the 1980s. I recorded two albums at the same time, one a live album, *Torch Songs and Some Not So Tortuous*, recorded as a live television special with a live audience at the Regent Hotel Supper Club by ABC TV and released as an album as well, and *Old Friends ... the Songs of Stephen Sondheim* later retitled *The Stephen Sondheim Songbook,* when released on CD. That TV special was a great privilege to do and to have as a record of a wonderful period of my career. It was fantastic to have my own television special produced. The first Sondheim album is an album of which I am very proud to this day.

Some years later, I released a Volume Two of the Sondheim album. I am proud of that as well. I still have the back-and-forth correspondence with Steve Sondheim about the second recording. We had sent him the album for his approval, before release. We had included two songs from his very early career, songs he had written while he was at college and which had been previously unrecorded. Steve objected to them being included and we cut them from the album immediately, as he wished.

We had also changed some of the harmonies in some of our arrangements, which he adamantly disagreed with. Composers, perhaps rightly so, are protective of their original harmonies and arrangements. Much correspondence ensued.

'Geraldine. Would you change other composers' arrangements or just mine?'

'I have changed many arrangements by many composers over the years,' I wrote back.

While it was my intention to always honour him and his material, I believed that if I simply sang the original Broadway arrangements there would be no reason for anyone to buy my record. I wasn't a famous recording artist like, say, Barbra Streisand, who could sell millions of albums, with the original arrangements. Steve had already cited her as an example of what he was speaking about.

'Barbra respects me. Why can't you, Geraldine?'

I didn't know whether to be flattered or upset.

I wanted a new feel to some of the songs to make them mine. Otherwise, why would people not just buy the original cast recording and leave it at that?

'Your voice will be the difference, Geraldine,' Steve wrote.

He believed my vocals should be the only change, with his preferred original arrangements remaining intact. In the end, we had to agree to disagree.

This album was followed up with more cast recordings over the next few years. New albums and many compilation discs were to come, culminating in my three-CD set for Désirée Records, in 2018, in the Great Australian Voices series.

At the time of recording the first Sondheim album, I had no idea that I was indeed the first artist in the world to record a solo Sondheim album – unbelievable really. It became quite a collector's item and sold well in the US and in the UK, as well as Australia. Michael Tyack was the musical director, with the fabulous Bill Motzing, among others, doing many of the orchestral arrangements.

Cleo Laine and Julie Wilson released Sondheim albums soon after mine. Then, Streisand released an album containing a great deal of Sondheim. I was surprised and elated to find myself on the cover of an American theatre magazine, with Steve Sondheim in the centre, and Julie Wilson, Cleo Laine and me surrounding him. We were described as 'Sondheim's Ladies'.

The 1980s also saw Kinselas, the old funeral parlour in Taylor Square in Sydney, open as a fantastic performance space. I performed in three very successful seasons at this most wonderful cabaret venue and restaurant. The bar on the second level was a hangout for actors, who would meet up after various shows and drink and laugh into the early hours. A huge photograph of me hung on the wall as you walked up the stairs. Other huge photos of Marcia Hines and Renée Geyer languished on the walls as well. When the venue was sold off years later, and everything was auctioned, I was happily surprised when Leon Fink, who had been one of the owners, delivered my photo to me in a truck. I was touched. It lives in my study, scarily big, but a wonderful reminder of a great period in Sydney cabaret. And it is a fantastic portrait, taken by the wonderful Stuart Campbell.

It seems that cabaret venues do well for a time, then they close. It is a great pity that they seem to be unsustainable. I hold out hope that Claire's Kitchen in Sydney, where I have performed a few shows, the most recent ones at the end of 2020 and in March 2022, remains successful. It is a wonderful French restaurant, and a cosy, sophisticated cabaret room. I love performing there.

My stage career took me back to the Sydney Theatre Company in 1985, creating the role of Mrs Yabsley in the new Australian musical, *Jonah Jones*. I loved being back at STC and was thrilled to be a part of this new Australian ensemble work, written by John Romeril and Alan John. This musical was directed by Richard Wherrett and played at The Wharf. I had been the first person to utter a sound at that theatre, when the Sydney Theatre Company had thrown a huge party for the opening of the wonderful wharf development, an idea of Neville Wran's. Robyn Nevin was the first to speak and I was the first to sing. We had been a part of that theatre family since the outset. Throughout those decades, working at the Sydney Theatre Company always felt like coming home.

One of the boys in the cast irritated me and I let him get to me during the production week. I recall being upset one day, as we were all standing on stage while lighting was happening around us. He made a quip and I said, 'I'm leaving.'

I walked off the stage, into the dressing room, already feeling a bit silly, threw everything into my makeup bag and began the long walk down the wharf towards my car.

For those of you who know that theatre, it is a long way to the street. I was about a third of the way, when I realised just how stupidly I was behaving. I turned around. I walked back to the dressing room. Put down my makeup bag, and returned to my position on stage, with everyone still standing there. I said, 'I never leave.'

Thankfully, everyone laughed and on we went with the rehearsal.

The following year, 1986, I played Joanne in *Company* at the Drama Theatre at the Sydney Opera House for Richard. Choreographed by Ross Coleman and designed by Brian Thomson, the old team from *Chicago* was back together again. This was the Australian premiere. We sold standing room each night. It was a stellar cast and we were a happy lot to have been given a gift like this Sondheim show to perform each night. I had listened to the Broadway cast recording for some time before we began rehearsals. I was shocked when I received the script and discovered that I had always misheard one of the lyrics of 'The Ladies Who Lunch'. In the song there is a lyric, 'I'll drink to that ... and one for Mahler!' I had always heard, 'I'll drink to that ... and one firm olive!' Made perfect sense to me.

I cannot express enough how fantastic it was to create roles and be a part of that creative process for so many musicals throughout this period of my career, from the 1980s into the 1990s at the Sydney Theatre Company, and many of them Australian premieres. While I have appeared, of course, in established Broadway productions, and have happily been allowed to put my own stamp on roles such as Reno Sweeney in *Anything Goes*, while working within an established production, I have also endured the 'McDonald's' musicals ... you know, the burger tastes the same everywhere. I understand creative teams guarding their productions, controlling everything, and wanting them reproduced exactly, but these absolute copies don't leave much room for an artist to bring individual presence to a show. You were not there for the creation, with the original director. You just have to work out a way to be yourself, to make the role yours, within the limits you are presented. With Disney taking over the world, this is becoming the norm.

There's also the fact that individual-sounding singing voices and styles have virtually disappeared. Everyone sounds the same as each other these days in musicals. If you close your eyes, you really can't tell who is singing. There is almost no character in the voice. It almost sounds like a cartoon voice. It has become the fashion to remove any sense of uniqueness. I find that a little sad, certainly boring. I long for the days of last century, when we were encouraged to be individuals. Still, now and again, an amazing, unique voice and talent breaks through and that is just wonderful.

When I was a young girl, we couldn't wait to see the latest musical from Broadway on stage, here in Australia, hear songs for the first time and love them. The anticipation of not knowing what you were about to see was such an exhilarating experience. Nowadays, it seems to me, particularly with the Disney repertoire, that all this has changed. A family goes to see the cartoon film. Buys all the memorabilia. Downloads the show. Watches it a hundred times. Knows every line. Then the 'on stage' version, with actors playing the roles arrives. Families attend, knowing every line, every song. They buy more memorabilia. Attending a musical is an entirely different experience.

There is nothing wrong with that. It is simply not the same.

Of course, there is always that breakthrough show that becomes a hit against the odds. There always will be, thankfully. This is the sort of show I tend to seek out. This is the sort of show I adore.

I do long for the day when we don't need a conversation about diversity on our stages and screens, that it just is. It's a no-brainer: of course, we should see more people of colour in leading roles, more LGBTQI people in leading roles, as well as performers with disabilities.

Sometimes, I love a classic revisited, with gender changes and same sex relationships replacing heterosexual relationships. At times, this can work really well and a show can be seen in a new light. However, I don't want to see every show for the next twenty years with such changes and I do have a problem with the notion that, for instance, you must be gay to play a gay role and so on.

I think that an actor's sexual preference is none of my business as an audience member. I just want to see great acting. I was following a thread on Facebook recently, where the casting of *The Sound of Music* was being discussed in these terms. I laughed out loud when a friend wrote, jokingly, 'Actors cast in the roles of Max and the Baroness must have lived experience of Austrian aristocracy.'

Is that where we are headed? A slippery slope, I would suggest.

In 1987, I did a tour of *HMS Pinafore*, my first role with Victoria State Opera. I played Buttercup, opposite my long-time friend, John O'May, who had starred in *Company*. The star of this show was the wonderful Paul Eddington, of *Yes, Minister* and *Robin Hood* fame. I had watched him play Will Scarlett in the TV series of *Robin Hood* as a child in Brisbane. Paul became a close friend during that tour and beyond, until his untimely death.

Paul was certainly one of the best people I have ever met in my life. He was a Quaker. After speaking with him a lot about Quakers, I know that, if there were any religion I could follow, it would be that one. (Mind you, there are always exceptions to any rule. Richard Nixon was a Quaker.) Paul was a pacifist, honest to a fault, with the most enviable integrity. And he was very funny and brilliant and wise and extremely kind.

We had a tough stage manager on that tour. In those days, actors, singers, dancers were fined for things like being late for the half-hour call and the money was taken out of your pay and sent to the Actor's Benevolent Fund. Well into the sold-out season, we had about twelve weeks of the show to go, some of the male dancers were running into the theatre just on or just after the half hour, to be greeted by the stage manager at stage door, looking at his watch and saying, 'You're late. You're fined.'

Tempers were frayed. The boys called a company meeting. They realised they were in the wrong, but felt that the fines were a step too far.

Finally, Paul suggested a solution. He said we should all contribute some money into a kitty; that the principals could afford to put in more. This money would be enough to cover any future fine until the end of the season and the remainder of the money could be used for a big party at the end of the tour. Then Paul went on to say, as only a Quaker would, 'Of course, all the money will be there at the end of the season to be spent on the party, as no-one will want to let us down.'

No-one was ever late again.

Paul ended up dying of a dreadful form of cancer, which ravaged his skin. There was evidence of it even then. He shared with me that he had had tests for the skin condition and was told that it was a form of cancer and that it would eventually develop and kill him. This he learnt on the day we opened in Brisbane. I knew, but not many others did, that Paul was in shock from this awful news as he made his first entrance as Sir Joseph Porter that opening night in Brisbane. He was flown in in a hot air balloon, a sensational entrance. He 'dried' in his number and just couldn't cover it. He received bad reviews for the only time on the tour. I wanted to shout to the rooftops the reason for his unsteady performance that night, but couldn't. Sometimes, critics are cruel and we just have to suck it up.

After this tour, I was offered the title role in the Offenbach operetta *La Belle Hélène* for Victoria State Opera and Mrs Lovett, in *Sweeney Todd* for Melbourne Theatre Company at the same moment. With the dates just lining up, and much negotiation, I was able to do both. How lucky I felt, as I would have hated not to be able to do *Sweeney Todd*.

As for *La Belle Hélène*, I did suggest at the time that opera critics may not like hearing a musical theatre voice in an Offenbach operetta, and as they had cast another music theatre voice, John O'May to play opposite me, this idea might prove challenging. They assured us both that that was what they wanted. It was an extremely 'camp' John Copley production. The rest of the principal cast was from the opera world.

As half expected, while I sang all of the notes, and acted the role well, my reviews were terrible, as were John's. They said we didn't have operatic voices. Well … yes … and? I shudder to think of those reviews. They were unwarranted. I did look gorgeous, with divine Kenneth Rowell costumes.

Sweeney Todd was a joy from start to finish. I played opposite Peter Carroll. Again, it was a very creative process. Strangely enough, two productions occurred at the same time. South Australian Opera had bought the South Australian rights for a large-scale operatic production, directed by Gale Edwards, with Lyndon Terracini and Nancye Hayes. I never saw it as we were playing at the same time in different cities.

Our production, directed by Roger Hodgman and choreographed by Garry Ginivan, was presented as a chamber piece, which I believe focused this story of obsession. I decided early on, as I was a little young to play Mrs Lovett at that time, that my character was obsessed sexually with Todd and this gave me the ability to give an individual reading of her, most unlike the original iteration, not at all a copy in any way of any other production. I remain very proud of this show. We ended up playing Melbourne at the Playhouse at the Arts Centre, Sydney at Her Majesty's Theatre (produced by Wilton Morley by then), and at Expo in Brisbane the following year on the River Stage to thousands of people.

During this season in Brisbane, darling Garry Ginivan, our wonderful choreographer, whom I had known since *Chicago*, got himself into a little bit of trouble. He had been out drinking after rehearsal. He caught a bus home to the house he had rented and got off the bus at the wrong stop. He knew he lived on the second street on the right from the bus stop, the fourth house on the left. In those days, many people in Queensland left their houses unlocked. So, Garry walked into the house he thought was his, into the kitchen, opened the fridge, got a beer out and sat down, turning the TV on.

The elderly couple, in bed at the time, woke up startled, screaming. There was a scene. The husband grabbed Garry and held him down and the wife called the police. It was all sorted eventually, but I don't think Garry ever caught the bus home again.

I performed four shows at Expo on the River Stage. The opening concert found me, as well as the dancers, arriving by boat, with some choreography on the boat, and the music and arrival timed to get us disembarked and on the River Stage at a certain musical point to continue the number. It was a fabulous Busby Berkeley kind of routine.

Then I did Queensland Day, where I played Golden Circle pineapple rings, I kid you not. My costume was ridiculous. I sang a medley of silly Australian songs. It was the only time in my career I have played a pineapple.

Then came *Sweeney Todd*, followed by a big concert I performed with an orchestra and dancers, called *Geraldine Turner Sings Australia*. It was all Australian songs, opening with a wonderful anthem-like arrangement of 'The Road to Gundagai'. Tony Sheldon was my guest. We did an hysterical potted version of an old Australian musical *Collits' Inn*, a show that Gladys Moncrieff had appeared in originally, with the two of us playing every character in the show in about five minutes! It was a concert of which I remain proud. Max Lambert was MD.

During the Melbourne rehearsal period of *Sweeney Todd*, I caught a cold and persistent cough that would not go away. After struggling for some time, I was eventually diagnosed with adult onset asthma and placed on steroids and a puffer that made my mouth very dry – the enemy of a singer. It took a while to get the balance of drugs right. I recall being very nervous on the opening night in Melbourne as my mouth kept becoming quite parched each time I began to sing. Also, it was not until the Sydney season that we had body microphones. We had to do the season in Melbourne with a few shotgun microphones across the front of the Playhouse stage. I felt like I was battling a war each night, as the musical is written, with the pithy lyrics, for body microphones. Still, we opened very well and did well.

I had always been an activist and had been opinionated about issues concerning Actors' Equity. I had been sitting on committees over the years, so when I was asked to become federal president of the union, I stepped up to the task. Down the track, I won the next election to the position. I have always been a political animal. I grew up in Queensland during the Bjelke-Petersen years and loathed the laws about students being arrested for forming protest groups and hated the list of historic buildings in Brisbane that were pulled down by that government. Wonderful historic buildings like the Bellevue Hotel and Cloudland, an old dance hall, disappeared overnight. I hate injustice and have always found it easier to fight on behalf of others rather than myself. I was flattered to be asked to become president and leapt at it, with my full commitment and energy.

Lionel Murphy, former attorney-general in the Whitlam government and High Court justice, died in 1986. Neville Wran, the New South Wales Premier, asked me to sing at his funeral and then, soon after I became president of the union, he asked if I would become a trustee of the Lionel Murphy Foundation, which gives domestic and overseas law and humanities scholarships each year to deserving postgraduate students. I accepted with trepidation, and pointed out to Mr Wran that I had no law experience and was not an academic. He said that did not matter; they needed a perspective like mine. My first meeting time arrived. I walked into the room to find the original trustees included Mr Wran as Chairman, Gough Whitlam, Manning Clark and Don Dunstan, among others.

I still sit on that committee and it is one of the most worthwhile experiences I have ever had the pleasure to be a part of. I am also proud of my years at Actors' Equity, where we became the first actors' union in the world to set up the pathway for a workable superannuation scheme for Australian performers under my tenure, and we stretched ourselves to buy the building in Redfern where MEAA (Media, Entertainment and Arts Alliance, which Equity became) still resides. That was a great decision, which Michael Crosby, one of the greats of the union, and I insisted on pursuing.

We opened *Sweeney Todd* in Sydney in early 1988, the bicentennial year, and the year I received an Order of Australia for services to the arts. I was quite young to receive such an award and thought my family might be a little proud. Typically, one of my sisters-in-law said, 'Are there higher awards than the one you are getting?'

'Well, yes,' I said.

'Well, if you're so good, why aren't you getting a higher one?'

I was used to that kind of backhanded remark from my family, but still, it was disappointing.

I played Gertrude Lawrence in *Noel and Gertie* for Wilton Morley in 1988 at The Wharf in Sydney. I have always adored the material of Noel Coward, and continue to include his songs in any concert I do, so this show, with Peter Carroll, was an absolute delight to play. It was directed by Jon Ewing and choreographed by Nancye Hayes.

Wilton shared with me a lovely story about his grandmother, Gladys Cooper, a wonderful actress whom I have adored for years. They were driving along a country road in England when he was a boy. Wilton was in the back seat, with older brother Sheridan, who in fact wrote *Noel and Gertie*. His father, Robert Morley, was in the front passenger seat and Gladys Cooper, his gran, was driving. Actually, they were all quite concerned as Gladys was weaving all over the road, oblivious to any impending danger. Thank goodness there wasn't much traffic about. Robert piped up, 'Mother, why don't you pull over and let me drive.'

Gladys exclaimed, 'Oh. Am I driving?'

Sheridan came out for our production week and many a night we had drinks and chats about all things theatrical. Wilton was producing two shows at the same time in Sydney. He had the first production in Australia of *Blood Brothers* on at the Seymour Centre, at the same time as *Noel and Gertie*. These two productions ended up being the last for Wilton in Australia. In fact, he left the country in some debt before our closing night. We didn't get paid for our final week. Even so, I liked Wilton.

Life was good. My relationship with Greg Jones continued. He was no longer working for the Labor Party, but instead, being a business consultant. I thought at the time that, although there were some niggling problems between us, we were fine. Things would work out.

We had bought and sold a few houses in the inner west of Sydney, before settling in a rather grand Victorian house in Petersham, dubbed 'The Consulate' by some friends. We entertained a great deal. We hosted many parties, catered lunches for up to sixty people. You'd think we had money to burn.

In fact, I never knew Greg's earnings, how much money he did or didn't have, or anything about his work really. Sounds ridiculous to admit that, but I had my own funds throughout those years so I never relied on his salary.

I earned well in the 1980s. An opportunity presented itself for a wonderful advertising deal, where I was on a retainer for a number of years. So, with that and my theatre, film, television and concert earnings, I was doing very well. Problem was, I never thought it would end, so I spent wildly on clothes, overseas trips, new cars, shouting people outrageously generous things, and the best of everything. Shades of my mother! I didn't think to save or to try to pay the huge mortgage off. I thought money would just keep pouring in. I lived in the moment, never thinking to plan for the future. Such was the eighties.

As the decade drew towards an end, I was cast in a commercial production of *Don's Party*, the David Williamson play at the Sydney Opera House, playing the wife of the divine Hugo Weaving, directed by Graeme Blundell. It was a lovely production of a fabulous play.

It was during that season, I auditioned for Reno Sweeney in *Anything Goes*, which I had seen in New York and hoped to be considered for. The Jerry Zaks production, directed in Australia by Philip Cusack, who became a lifelong friend and who had also directed *They're Playing Our Song* out here, was to open in 1989 at The State Theatre in Sydney, with a tour to follow. I got the part.

11

Always True to You in My Fashion

It is the week after the opening night of Anything Goes. *We open really well. It is a personal triumph. Greg goes away for a couple of days on business. I decide to stay for a couple of nights at the Hilton Hotel, which is around the corner from the State Theatre, allowing me to catch up on rest.*

Greg comes back home from the business trip and calls me after the show. It is a great chat. I feel close to him again. He expects me home tomorrow. I decide to surprise him. I drive home, put the key in the door, to find Greg, naked in the hallway looking sheepish.

He says, 'This is not a good time to come home.'

My stomach falls to the floor. I can't speak. I look ashen.

Greg says, 'Could you leave for a while, maybe drive around the neighbourhood for about twenty minutes while I get rid of her?'

I do it.

I drive around, doing 'humping crying'. I get back. Greg puts the kettle on. I ask, 'How long has this been going on?'

'Three years.'

People at the theatre the next night ask me why I didn't burst into the room to see

who it is. I can't answer that. Fear that it could be someone I know? Down the track,
I find out it is a friend of mine, who had been in a financial crisis a few years before.
So I suggested she move into our spare room at our former home, not pay any rent,
just get herself sorted. Seems she did that all right.

I tell our Portuguese cleaner, Isabelle, the next day. She says, 'I know you away.
I feel sorry for him. I wash everything for when he get back. Change the bed for him.
Iron the doona cover so it nice for him. Clean everything. Tidy bedroom. But if I
know he do this, I shit on doona!'

ی

Anything Goes was the most fabulous Cole Porter show, filled with great performers, colleagues and much happiness.

During one of our previews, Simon Burke and I were in the middle of 'You're the Top' in Act One, when it came over a loudspeaker that everyone was to vacate the theatre. Turned out it was a bomb scare. I remember the cast over the road from the State Theatre, outside the Queen Victoria Building in our gorgeous costumes, mingling with audience members, wondering what this night would hold. We were let back in to the theatre about an hour or more later, after the bomb squad had done its thing. Most of the audience returned and we began our number again and went on from there.

Greg and I stayed together, but the relationship was broken. I began an affair that was both exciting and unhealthy for me. Really, my problem was my relationship with Greg, which limped along till 1991. I was simply avoiding facing it.

My emotions were all over the place during the season. At times, I reminded myself of my mother, with my insecurities. A few years later, I found out from a doctor, after I met my husband Brian and tried in vain to have a child, that I had been going through a very early menopause (from thirty-eight to forty-three), which started during *Anything Goes*, hence the emotional roller-coaster.

Nevertheless, I remained at the peak of my power as a performer. It was an absolute gift of a part and the role fitted me like a glove. In fact, recently, I was listening to a podcast (one of the series, *Stages* by my friend Peter Eyers) where I heard the person being interviewed talk about my performance as Reno Sweeney being the reason he went into the theatre. He said I played it as if it were the last show I was ever going to do. Makes it all worthwhile to hear that.

I recall one matinee day. It must have been early in the second season at the State Theatre, as darling Philip Cusack, our wonderful director was still here. He was a very good friend of Lorna Luft's. Her sister, Liza Minnelli, was in Sydney doing a concert tour with Sammy Davis Junior and Frank Sinatra. Liza had invited Philip to stand in the wings and watch their show. He told me he saw just how much Frank was the boss. After a huge ovation, Sammy and Liza wanted to go back for yet another curtain call, maybe another encore, but Frank walked past them and said gruffly, 'It's over.'

No-one said anything and they all returned to the dressing rooms. That was that. He who must be obeyed had spoken.

Anyway, Sammy and Liza came to our matinee that week. I didn't meet them, as they had to rush back to their hotel to prepare for a show that evening. Liza did send me a box of chocolates, Cadbury's Roses, backstage, with a lovely note.

We played two Sydney seasons, as well as Melbourne, Brisbane, Adelaide and New Zealand. We opened in 1989 and played through till 1991. I adored it. We also recorded a great cast album.

When I won the Performer of the Year award for playing Reno Sweeney, I knew Gough Whitlam, former prime minister, former trustee of the Lionel Murphy Foundation and fierce defender of the arts, and his wife, Margaret, were in the audience. I dedicated my award to him and told the audience that he was my hero. Gough walked to the front of the stage and knelt at my feet. I was really moved. He had already attended the show, had visited my dressing room and had drunk champagne from my shoe! Surely that is a first.

The other memorable thing about that first Sydney season of *Anything Goes* was meeting one of my nephews for the first time. My brother Leigh had married when he was nineteen. That marriage didn't last. Leigh had not escaped the trauma from our family dynamic. I think that's why he had married at such a young age. Leigh says that he remembers hardly anything from his childhood. It was obviously as difficult for him as it was for me to be a part of such a dysfunctional lot. His way of dealing with it was to block it all out, to disengage emotionally, to not be present in that house of ours. He started a relationship with his now wife, Nerida, while still technically married.

She got pregnant. None of us knew. In fact, Mum had died never knowing she had another grandson. Nerida came from a rather conservative family so it was decided that they would go to New Zealand. Turns out they didn't know if they would stay together, so they gave the baby up for adoption, much to their regret. Fast-forward the years, and they registered to find him when he came of age, hoping he'd do the same. Well, they found him.

His family, his mum and dad and brother, lovely people whom I met later, when we toured New Zealand with the show, really embraced the situation and have been totally conciliatory and kind and understanding.

One night during our run in Sydney, Leigh and Nerida brought Seumas to the show. My dressing room was at the bottom of the stairs at the State Theatre. It was amazing to see a tall, lanky young man, who walked and gestured and smiled like my father, walk down those stairs and enter my dressing room. It was quite extraordinary to meet someone for the first time and yet feel a familiar sense of family. Seumas later moved to Perth, where Leigh and Nerida live, and he now has three children of his own. We see each other when we can. Sometimes life delivers you happy and unexpected surprises.

My friendship with Philip Cusack continued. Every time I was in New York, we saw each other a great deal. We spoke very regularly. He also directed *Lost In Yonkers* for the Sydney Theatre Company. So indeed, we saw a lot of him over the years. We spent many Christmases together and shared much.

He was hit by a van in New York in June 2013, a freak accident. He was in hospital, recovering, when he took a sudden turn for the worse and died. I was devastated, especially as I had not seen him in a while. Philip was a truly remarkable person.

When I would come up with an alternative idea for a scene in rehearsal, I can still hear him saying, 'Get your own play.' Then he'd throw his head back and laugh. I absolutely adored him.

He knew all those old tricks of the theatre. He always, for instance, insisted on the air conditioning being turned down a couple of notches on opening nights. He said that audiences always laugh more if they are a little cooler. It makes sense when you're doing a comedy to have your audience attentive and ready to laugh. How many times have you felt too hot in a theatre and almost nodded off?

And Philip always brought down the lights on stage ever so slightly before my first entrance. Then he would boost the lights, adding a dome, as I entered. This could lead people, including critics, to say things like, 'As she entered, she lit up the stage'.

Fabulous. I really miss him in my life.

At the end of 1990, Wayne Harrison became the new artistic director of Sydney Theatre Company, with Richard's departure, after ten years at the helm. Wayne asked me to sit on the Board. It was customary to include an actor on the Board of Sydney Theatre Company. Wayne and I had been close friends for years. We went way back to *No, No, Nanette* days, where his mantra, as a performer was, 'You have to steal a little bit extra every night.'

I totally disagree with that but have never forgotten him saying it.

That reminds me of what I call 'The Connie Hobbs Factor'.

Connie Hobbs was a character actor of the old school, who had played in *Irene* for J. C. Williamson's amongst many other roles. Pamela Gibbons who was in that cast, complained to me at the time about the fact that Connie used to get a huge round of applause after almost all her exits, by pulling a face out front and doing a 'silly comedy walk' off. Also, her curtain call always received a huge reaction.

Now, let me say that I am not being disparaging of Connie. That was a choice in the old days, a way of playing, of stealing a little bit extra every night!

Pamela couldn't believe that the rest of the cast was busy doing the triple threat thing each night, and acting up a storm, while Connie simply entered, pulled a face, then exited with a funny walk ... and received a huge reaction.

I said to Pamela what I often say, 'You can pick your nose on stage and get a laugh. Doesn't make it right.'

I went on to say that I'll bet the audience, while having a cup of tea or drink after the show at home or chatting about the show the next morning at breakfast, talk about Julie Anthony's performance as Irene, or Pamela's, or Noel Ferrier's, or any of the other fabulous principal players. It is not always the quick fix thrill of the person who gets the easy laugh that is the lasting memory of a show. It is the star performances that remain in people's hearts long after the curtain has fallen.

I told Pamela not to worry about 'The Connie Hobbs Factor'. Let her have her moment. Good for her! No harm in that!

I do think Wayne changed his tune over the years about stealing a little bit extra every night.

Wayne wanted to open his first season at STC in 1991 with *Kiss Me Kate*, the wonderful Cole Porter musical, starring Philip Quast and me. We had a meeting, but Philip was not interested. I don't think he ever shared with us his reason for not wanting to do it. It wasn't until a couple of years later that we worked together. It would have been a fine part for him. Pity. What might have been?

Instead, Wayne decided to open his first season with *A Little Night Music*, with me as Desirée and John Waters as Fredrik. It was utter joy. I hadn't worked with John for ages.

I did still have commitments with *Anything Goes* in Auckland, so it was organised for me to open and play the first few weeks in Auckland, then fly back, rehearse Desirée in Sydney during the week, then fly back to play weekend performances of Reno Sweeney in Auckland, leaving the last couple of weeks in Auckland for my cover to take over as Reno, as we moved into production week in Sydney at STC.

I remember doing a publicity interview in Auckland with wet, straggly hair – most unbecoming for a leading lady. I was staying in a rather posh hotel and was getting dressed for the interview downstairs in a room off the lobby, when I attempted to use the hair dryer in my very expensive room. It worked for a short amount of time then cut out. I called reception and asked for a replacement dryer as this one had cut out while I was trying to dry my hair. The receptionist didn't suggest they would send a replacement at all. Rather, she chastised me. Seems it was my fault the dryer had cut out. 'Your heer's too thuck.'

We played *A Little Night Music* at the Drama Theatre at Sydney Opera House and sold out. There was talk of a transfer to the Theatre Royal, but John Waters wasn't available, so it didn't go ahead.

After the first preview, I returned home to Petersham to Richard Wherrett's fiftieth birthday party. He had organised for several friends to give dinner parties. He attended each of them and then they all ended up at the 'Consulate,' for the big birthday bash later that evening.

When I walked in, tired from the whole production week and first show with an audience, I wasn't allowed in my bathroom. There was a guard of sorts on the door. That room, it turned out, had been set up as the 'drugs' room. The house was brimming with people, so full I couldn't see anything of the house. There were hundreds of people there. It was a rainy night. The house had a white tiled floor (I know, it was an eighties renovation, okay?) so you can imagine the amount of mud being ground into the floor, along with much broken glass.

People were naked in the pool. There was a wonderful moment when the cake, which must have cost a fortune and was a copy of the shape of the tattoo Richard had given himself for his birthday, the shape of a lightning rod, sitting on a huge glass base, was carried by a few queens around by the pool. Of course, they slipped and dropped it and broke into floods of laughter. The glass base shattered into the cake mixture. They left it where it fell, as others started to sing, 'Someone left the cake out in the rain ...'

At that point, I took to my bed. I was exhausted. Many people sat on my bed and we all laughed and told stories till the early hours. I have no idea what time the last person left, but the sun was up. One partygoer fell against every poster in the hallway and smashed the glass in each of the frames on his way out. Yes. He was as drunk as that. I had agreed to the party because Richard promised he would have cleaners come the next day and I would never know there had been a party.

So, to my surprise, as I made coffee and surveyed the damage and the former white floor, caked with mud, looking like a brown floor, and mess ... oh the mess ... the doorbell rang.

'Great. The cleaners have arrived.'

Remember I had another preview performance in a few hours.

I opened the door to find a really scrawny young man, smiling as he said, 'I'm the cleaner.'

I anticipated a team of professional cleaners. 'Where's your equipment?' I said, as I expected industrial cleaning equipment. Of course, he had none.

So, I spent the day helping this lovely young man to try to get the house in some sort of order. Richard and a few friends arrived to help mid-afternoon, but only managed a swim in the pool. They were tired. Poor things. Big night. Well, what about me, with a show to do?

I remember one matinee day of *A Little Night Music* … why is it always matinee days? There was an accident with one of the dome operators. In those days, harnesses were not a requirement. After this particular day, it became mandatory at the Opera House. This young woman had complained that she had been up all night the night before with nausea. She hadn't eaten. By the time she climbed up into position to operate the spotlight, she felt unwell but talked on 'the cans' to stage management and said she thought she could get through it.

We started the show. It is comforting that you tend to repeat things absolutely backstage during a performance. I love that familiar routine you fall into. Changes become streamlined. Conversations with other performers happen at the same time each night. It is all part of the backstage choreography.

John and I had completed the first part of the 'Digs' scene in Act One, where Madame Armfeldt, played by the wonderful Bettina Welch, enters and sings 'Liaisons'.

John and I always had our customary chat in the wings during this song, while our dressers fussed.

Suddenly, we heard a thud, followed by the music stopping and our stage manager walking on stage to ask if there was a doctor in the house. Then we heard loud groaning, really unnerving.

The young, unwell woman had fainted, and fallen out of her perch onto the floor of the theatre during Bettina's song. Of course there were doctors in the house. There always are.

The audience was led out and given cups of tea. An ambulance was called. We went back to our dressing rooms, thinking the rest of the show would be cancelled, surely. The unnerving groans continued over the loud speakers. After she had been taken away in an ambulance with serious head injuries (thankfully, she made a full recovery) we received word from Wayne Harrison that we were to go on, beginning with Bettina's number.

The audience came back in. The stage manager walked on and explained that the young woman was fine now and at the hospital in good hands. The audience accepted that and applauded. We were worried that the next part of our scene, which is pure comedy, would die a natural death. However, the first laugh was huge. I think it was relief for everyone. It had been the right decision to continue.

But the most extraordinary thing was that it turned out the young woman in question, and her brother, an opera singer, used to be babysat by my mother in Brisbane when they were little. This was incredible, surprising news. I knew in her later life, Mum used to earn some extra cash babysitting but this coincidence was too much. Talk about six degrees of separation! It seems there is no escaping my mother, even now, so many years after her death. Who am I kidding? Escape? She is an ever-present force in my life.

It was during this season I found out that Bill Shanahan was ill. He had thrown me the most fantastic fortieth birthday party the year before. He knew then that he had AIDS. I had no idea. I had turned forty in Adelaide, during *Anything Goes*, where producer Jon Nichols had thrown a soiree for me after the show. So kind.

Simon Burke, Tom Blair, and Glenn Flavin, friends from the cast had taken me on 'a secret destination tour' that morning in a limo. For weeks they had left cryptic notes about me having to be in the foyer of my hotel at a given time on the day for a mystery outing. My birthday was a Saturday, a matinee day.

I was convinced that we were going to a sausage sizzle. Why? I have no idea. I kept saying to them, 'I know we're going to a sausage sizzle. We're not going to the hills are we? We're not having croissants are we?'

Shut up, girl. Be grateful.

We ended up at a restaurant, you guessed it, in the hills, with champagne and croissants. It was so lovely of them and it turned out to be great fun.

I had begun that show at thirty-eight. I hated turning forty. But that party of Bill's was exceptional and took away the sting of becoming so 'old'. It was at his house, a few weeks after my birthday. We had lost many friends to AIDS in the eighties. I was so shocked to find out that my darling friend was very ill during that *A Little Night Music* run. We closed after a hugely successful, extended season.

Suddenly, it was hospital visits, worry, trying to be cheerful, hoping that he would continue to fight. Then the day came where I visited Bill and could see that he was tired. He told me he didn't want any more treatment. He said, 'We have to be brave, darling.' I didn't want to be. I couldn't bear the thought of life going on without him.

There were few of us, the inner circle, who knew the truth. Bill had stepped back from the agency. Most of the actors thought he was having a break and would return. The inner circle knew better and we kept up a roster, visiting him, just being there, talking if he wanted to, watching television together if he wanted to. I was on the roster, years later, when we sat with darling Richard Wherrett as he faded away from liver disease. Awful.

It was only a matter of weeks Bill spent at home. When he died, he did look peaceful and beautiful. All the pain in his face had disappeared. He became younger looking. He became Bill again. We dressed him in his favourite suit, laughing at times, as his lifeless body didn't do what we wanted it to. It was surreal, as our darling friend was zipped up into a body bag and taken away and reality hit.

The funeral was huge. Bill was much loved by the entire industry. In fact, unlike most agents these days who only seem to like and support their own clients, Bill would sometimes suggest to producers that someone else from another agency would be perfect for the part in question. Such was his absolute honesty and integrity. He was held in high esteem.

White flowers, his choice, flooded the enormous entrance to the church and poured down the steps onto the footpath, so much so that there was hardly room to walk. I remember Mel Gibson lurking at the back of the church – standing room only – as Bill had been responsible for his career, as well as countless others. There were readings, Shakespeare sonnets, songs and music. I did a reading and it was incredibly sad and numbing.

We all got through the day somehow.

I stayed at the agency for three more years, but it was never the same for me without Bill at the helm. A few of the friends I thought I knew, had always spent Christmas with, had seen every week, and had shared much with, drifted away as I slowly realised that Bill had been the glue. Bill had kept us together. Now that he was gone, those supposed friendships were gone. That was a really deep disappointment.

I miss him every day of my life. I think of him every day of my life. This was a friendship that was pure love, a friendship that endures to this day and he is ever present in all that I do, in all that I am. He left me some money, as he did for others, and the most fantastic seascape painting by Jani Pohl, which sits on my living room wall and will travel with me to any home I live in. More than that, he left me with my ever-present memories of him and what feels like a lifetime of laughter and love. For me, there is life before Bill, life with Bill and life after Bill. That is all.

Greg didn't come to the funeral. He was away on business.

Not long after Bill died, I had to do a season at the Tilbury Hotel, a great venue in Sydney's inner city. I had done several shows there. I developed a cold and my voice was hoarse, but I soon realised this was grief and panic manifesting itself. There was nothing wrong with my voice. It was my heart that was broken. I kept postponing the opening until I couldn't any more. I remember the torture of trying to sing each night at home and my voice not obeying me. I had always been that girl with the big voice, that girl whose voice could do what it was told.

I tell this story to students, if I ever take master classes. It turned out to be a pivotal moment in my performing life. Singing is an emotional as well as a technical thing. For instance, if that big note is coming up and you think you might not hit it, you can bet your bottom dollar you won't. It is a question of having the confidence, knowing absolutely that all those notes are there at your command.

For the first time in my life, my confidence drained from me. Not even 'I am beautiful. I am talented. I have a secret' worked. As a last resort, I joked more with the audience. I brought more of 'me' forward, as I simply had to get through each night. Many people during that season said that they thought it was the best I had ever performed. I was forced to think about that. I mean, sometimes I went for a note and nothing came out. Sometimes I was like the old me and sang very well. I just never knew, from moment to moment, which would come out, the great vocal or the not so great vocal. And yet, something was different. I was in the moment, flying without a harness.

I had long known that it was not all about the voice or what a performer does technically. Otherwise every ensemble member, with a great voice, would be a star. It is about what a performer has to say. I had long known that if I had gone to see a famous ballerina like, say, a Margot Fonteyn and she had fallen out of a pirouette that I would not love her any less. She was, after all, more than the sum of her parts.

This was the epiphany. Could it be that they liked me, not just my voice? Honestly, that had never occurred to me. I realised in that instant, that I had been hiding all these years behind my big voice that always did what it was told.

I say to young performers that, although, of course, we want to achieve great vocals, we want to strive to achieve technical perfection, it is of the utmost importance that we find out who we are and what we have to say. That is what audiences respond to. That is what separates us from the rest and makes us special.

The 'fear' as I call it, continues to live with me since that time. I have struggled with it on many occasions, especially for the decade after Bill died. These days, however, things are better. I mostly win. I know the 'fear' is still there, just lurking beneath the surface, waiting for any minor criticism, for a missed laugh from an audience, for an indifferent round of applause, any small gap so it can crawl out of the darkness into the light. It is bubbling away underneath the surface, waiting for a chink so it can emerge. The best thing I can do is embrace the randomness of performing, rely on my technique and know it is there, dig deep, forgive myself for imperfections and, above all, always, always be in the moment.

12

The Gypsy in Me

It is the Thursday before Good Friday in 1992. We have been rehearsing Gypsy for a week. The ensemble is to join next week, after the Easter break. We are opening at Her Majesty's Theatre in Sydney, rehearsing in the Betty Pounder Rehearsal Rooms. I notice my wallet has been stolen and report it to the police. It is found later in a bin at Town Hall station, with all the contents removed. It is a favourite wallet, so this must be a good omen. In fact, this is the third time this wallet has been stolen and returned. The first was in New York, sent back by NY's finest police department. It is the first present I give my future husband after our marriage at the end of the following year: that lucky Il Bisonte wallet. He still has it.

Greg Jones is producing this show for me. However, we have broken up by now, and it is acrimonious, as he has left me for a nineteen-year-old, whom he later marries and has children with. Mind you, I have married by then. I believe he is given the rights to the show more easily as the company producing it is named B. Ellistock and Bloom (funny reference to The Producers), but surely this is a sign for things to come!

These are the days when you get your pay in brown pay packets with cash inside. I stay after rehearsal to get my cash, as everything has been stolen and I need the cash for the long weekend. A few others stay. We have a drink, hoping our money will appear. It is getting late when our wonderful stage manager, Gail Esler, decides to go across the road to the management office to see what is happening.

She returns about two hours later, with a few pay packets. She says she saw a limo pull up and a tall woman in stilettos emerge with a large brown paper bag. Gail follows her into the office, where this woman tips up the contents of the bag onto a desk and cash falls out.

So, those who remain, including Richard Wherrett, our director, are paid for the week's work. The others are not. By Tuesday morning, the show is cancelled. My agent lets me know. The newspapers report that I go to Greg's office and trash it. Never happened.

I do go there. I am furious. I walk into his office and shout, 'And where was the phone call from you, you prick?'

I think that is fair, after almost a decade living together. Then I see some papers on his desk, throw them in the air and walk out. If that is the definition of trashing, then so be it.

❧

This was the beginning of my ongoing relationship with *Gypsy* and the unprecedented cancellations to follow.

The Production Company, which provided some wonderful performances of musicals over the years, started up in 1999. In their first year, casual discussions took place about a production of *Gypsy* for me. It didn't end up being included in their program that year for some reason; they went in another direction. So imagine my surprise, towards the end of that year, before the announcement of their next season, when I received a phone call from an old friend asking me if I had heard that The Production Company was doing *Gypsy* the following year, starring Judi Connelli. My stomach immediately dropped to the floor. I was hurt and felt overlooked and disrespected.

Contrary to industry folklore, my upset over the casting of Rose had nothing to do with Judi. We had known each other since our teens, both being Brisbane girls, and had been up against each other for certain shows over the years. We had been in *Chicago* together and had performed in many concerts together starting back in the Bernard King days. A few years earlier, we had appeared in *Into the Woods* in the premiere production in Australia at the Sydney Opera House. By that time, a fictitious feud had been created in certain circles. Some people love to create drama and they imagine that two strong, female performers must hate each other. Certain folk took sides over the years. If you were a fan of mine, you couldn't possibly be a fan of hers and vice versa. It was simply ridiculous. So, I wished Judi well in the role, even though it was a long-held desire of mine to do the show. My sense of abandonment was aimed clearly towards the management.

I wrote a note to them asking if they thought my talent had disappeared over the last year and, if so, when in that year did that happen? I had held out hope that the project would go ahead sometime, with me in it. Was I crazy to think that within a few months, they had found cause to dump me? Of course, they had made their choice and that was that.

To their credit, they did ask me for a short list of shows I would like to do. I sent that off. The list included *Call Me Madam* and, again, to their credit, The Production Company included it in the same season as *Gypsy*, their second year of production.

Call Me Madam turned out to be the only show I was ever asked to do for that company, which produced shows for two decades. Although, some years later, they did ask me to appear in a featured, though not what would be considered a major role, or even a major featured role, in *Follies*.

I wrote another note. Seems I can't help myself. In it, I said that, after my particular career and knowledge of Sondheim, my Sondheim albums and the many Sondheim shows I had appeared in, mostly premieres in Australia, that the part offered to me was just not good enough for me to accept and I was fine about turning it down. I knew the major roles, even the major featured roles, were already cast.

I received a note back stating that most of the cast was simply happy to be a part of it, no matter which role they had been offered, and therefore they couldn't understand my stance. I wrote back saying that was not so for me. I suppose they thought I had ideas above my station, or, as I heard back from others, that I thought I was still young enough to be playing roles I was, in their view, too old to play. The leading roles in *Follies* are written for older actors, for God's sake.

I knew I had done my dash with them. There were many roles I could have been offered over the subsequent years. The Production Company was responsible for some wonderful shows that otherwise may very well not have graced our stages and gave a lot of opportunities to many terrific performers over those years. I was simply not one of them.

Robyn Nevin became artistic director of Sydney Theatre Company in 1999. In 2002, she called me in for a meeting and said she had plans to do a production of *Gypsy* in the following year's season for me. She would direct. I was elated. Surely, this was it. It was Sydney Theatre Company, after all, and it would certainly happen. In fact, it was to be a co-production with John Frost. Even better … of course it would happen!

The Helpmann Awards had recently started, so it was decided I would sing 'Rose's Turn' at the awards that year as a kind of promotion. I did and it was great to do it with an orchestra. I had recorded 'Everything's Coming up Roses' with an orchestra, way back when Greg Jones was producing the show for me, before the whole thing was aborted. That recording had been a free hand out, a promotion, connected to a magazine cover and featured interview.

So, a couple of weeks before the announcement of the 2003 season of STC, I heard the bad news. It turned out that Sam Mendes had bought the world rights that year for his upcoming production for Bernadette Peters on Broadway. Sydney Theatre Company thought getting the rights would be a simple task and had been stymied at the last hurdle.

I was devastated. *Gypsy* production number three had been a non-starter. This show kept eluding me.

After licking my wounds and going to ground for a while, I came up for air and decided to get on with my life, my career, to focus on my equilibrium and realise that the words *Gypsy* and Geraldine Turner do not belong in the same sentence.

Of course, I know that woman, Rose. She is my mother. I have always known that I could nail that part. The loss she feels is the loss my mother always felt about her life. I know it. I have seen and lived it. Of course, circumstances were completely different, but I knew that woman, a woman who wants something so much that she will do anything, give up anything, say anything, create any drama, live vicariously through her daughter to feel some sense of achievement in her otherwise unremarkable life. I certainly have the vocal ability to sing the show, the comedy timing for the role. Also, I believe I could bring some sex to the role, which I think is missing from some productions, the most recent ones particularly. The reason, for instance, I loved Tyne Daly so much in her interpretation on Broadway is just that. She is a wonderful actress, she could sing it, and you believed the depth of her relationship with Herbie. Therefore giving him up in Act Two was all the more poignant. She was a sensational Rose. It remains one of the best things I have ever seen. Patti LuPone was also a great Rose. Similarly, she brought sexiness and authenticity to the role and believability in the relationship with Herbie. I do wish I had seen Ethel Merman in the original production. Sadly, it was before my time.

So, onward … without *Gypsy!*

Then, blow me down, in 2017, I have been playing and touring my one-woman show, *Turner's Turn*, when I get a call from Jay James-Moody, who runs a small, independent company in Sydney, called Squabbalogic. Sometimes they present a one-off reading of a musical, a mystery show that punters buy tickets for, not knowing what the show will be; a good gimmick for a fundraiser! He asks me to play Rose in *Gypsy*, in one of these mystery musicals. No money, but what the hell, it is a one-off. Why not? This may be it, the one chance to play Rose.

My colleague and friend from *Anything Goes*, Simon Burke, is to play Herbie. Simon and I met with the musical director and we spent a lovely day, singing through the score. Rehearsals were set for a few weeks time. I went on with my tour, with plenty of time on my return for rehearsals and the performance. We would be off book for the numbers. That's fine. I have known them for years. I could do the songs in my sleep. I have loads of history and baggage to bring on stage with me. I found myself really looking forward to it.

I had some dates of my one-woman show in Melbourne. I was in a taxi going to a rehearsal with my producer, Enda Markey, when my phone rang. It was Jay James-Moody. When he said who it was, I asked jokingly, 'You're calling to tell me *Gypsy* has been cancelled, aren't you?'

I laughed. But no laughter came back at me down the phone line.

Instead, there was silence on the end of the phone! My stomach almost fell out as I said, 'You've got to be kidding. You are kidding, right?'

Jay said that, unfortunately, someone had reported that he didn't have the rights sewn up properly, so the show had to be cancelled. I have my suspicions about who reported it. He apologised profusely for doing this to me. I have no doubt he felt terrible and that his apology was genuine. He knew my history with this show. But what is this about rights and offering a show to someone without having the deal sewn up? Not good enough really.

By now, there was buzzing in my head, and I felt like throwing up, so I became very quiet. He asked if I'd like to do *Hello, Dolly!* instead. I have always wanted to play Dolly, but couldn't compute the offer at that very minute.

I said, 'Well, I would love to play Dolly sometime.' But then I said, 'No thanks.'

I just couldn't. I was too shattered. I was surprised how much this cancellation affected me. I guess I had thought, well, maybe I'll do the show just once. That will do. Yes. That will do. But the rug had been pulled out from under me ... again! How could this have happened? How could this keep on happening? *Gypsy* and Geraldine Turner do not belong in the same sentence.

It was a year later that Rodney Delaney, who had been one of the creators of The Actor's Company in Sydney years earlier, asked me if I would play Rose in a pro/am production of *Gypsy* in Queanbeyan, a city just outside Canberra, at their performing arts centre, run by council. He would direct. He had directed for them before and assured me that their presentations were of a high standard.

This production was to have happened two years earlier. The contract had been drawn up. Monies decided. Dates finalised. Then, out of the blue, Rodney called me and said that the council had been changed, or amalgamated, and that the new council was not willing to go ahead with the production at that time. So, if you count that failed starter, there have been six productions cancelled altogether. Unbelievable.

I had only ever performed in Queanbeyan a few decades before at the

School of Arts Cafe, which was a great cabaret venue run for a number of years by Bill Stephens. Over the years, he had continued to give a lot of opportunities to performers from all over Australia. I tried out many shows there and I believe there are some released recordings from that time, which marks another fabulous period of creativity in Queanbeyan. Bill Stephens was responsible for much of that.

In any case, with *Gypsy* I knew that Rodney would be committed to making me look good and I liked his ideas for the proposed production. He adored the show and really wished to enable me to play Rose. I was thankful for that.

I had never appeared in a community theatre production. Of course, I would be paid, quite well in fact, as it turned out. I did have some knowledge of community theatre as I had agreed to be the patron of Miranda Musical Society some years earlier and had mentored some of the younger performers there and directed a couple of shows for them, *Jacques Brel is Alive and Well and Living in Paris*, which had transferred to Riverside Theatre and had completed a small tour, and later, my production of *Les Misérables*, which sold out to much acclaim. So, I knew that this would involve night rehearsals, no problem. I simply had to get my head around being a professional actress in a community theatre show. I knew this would be my last bite at the apple as well. My management was on board with all of this as the money was quite good, the production team professional and so I was encouraged to agree to do it.

Rodney wanted them to sell the show with publicity that centred on 'At last, Geraldine Turner in *Gypsy!*' He hoped they would try to sell it interstate, as, by now, there would be a lot of people around the country who would wish to see me play it.

So, I agreed. Community theatre. There will be no problem with this being cancelled. They don't even have to pay a lot of the cast. This will surely go ahead.

I drove down for callbacks, particularly for Louise and Herbie, as the chemistry had to be right. We cast fantastic actors. I was happy and looked forward to the season and to starting rehearsals.

We had a launch of the 2019 season of the Queanbeyan Performing Arts

Centre, including a launch for our show. I sang 'Everything's Coming up Roses' at one of them, and at the full launch, I spoke. I remember saying that my life had come full circle. After five non-starters of this show, I felt I was absolutely ready to play this iconic role and that now was the perfect time in my life to do so. Many friends and fans had booked from Melbourne, Sydney, Brisbane and Canberra. It was an exciting time.

Rodney wanted to have a reading and a get-together a few weeks before starting rehearsals. We broke bread together and it was an altogether fantastic evening of a cast bonding. I looked forward to seeing several friends from interstate, who had booked flights already.

I had stayed out of little murmurings about Rodney and the council disagreeing about certain production values and the casting of the children, which was not complete. None of this was my business anyway and I was sure everything would be sorted. I found myself becoming really excited about playing Rose at last. Also, there was less pressure somehow in it not being a mainstream production in a major city. After my history with this show, I looked forward to feeling a sense of freedom to create my Rose, and to be able to concentrate on the 'work'.

A little over two weeks before we started rehearsals, I received a call from one of the councillors who ran the Queanbeyan Performing Arts Centre. He told me that they had fired Rodney Delaney from the project. I immediately asked if it was still going ahead and was assured that it was and they were trying to find a replacement director. I hung up, feeling a little empty and worried and called Rodney straight away.

He said that the council was hysterical about the fact that he had not cast all of the children yet. He did not see this as a problem, as the main children were cast and he was confident that he would cast the others before rehearsals started. He was about to audition at local dance schools.

Also, they were at loggerheads about the set build, which Rodney felt sure could be sorted. They disagreed and removed him from the project. Rodney tried to reassure me. I didn't really want a director of their choice coming on board. One of my reasons for agreeing to do it at all was that I knew that Rodney would always have my best interests at heart.

I hung up from him and called my agent, who put forward a couple of his stable of directors to the council. This made my mind settle. Having a professional director on board, a director who knew the show, and the history of it, was vital.

The very next day, two weeks before rehearsals were to begin, I received a call from the same councillor. He said, 'We have decided to cancel the production. It is too hard. But you are a lovely lady and it was very nice to meet you.'

Then he hung up, without giving me a chance to speak.

So this is how it ends, I thought. This whole saga of six cancellations of productions of *Gypsy* ends with, 'You are a lovely lady and it was very nice to meet you.' Clunk!

I wasn't upset. I was numb, I think. After all, I was used to it. I half expected it. Others were upset on my behalf, and angry for me. I'll never know what really happened behind the scenes. I believe the council had not realised just how big a show it is. I think they were probably underfunded. After speaking to the costume designer, wonderful Anna Senior, who told me she could not get a budget out of them, this makes sense. Rodney Delaney was merely collateral damage. No use worrying about what might have been.

I have not sung anything from *Gypsy* since and I don't intend to.

I rallied – after a period of grieving. I had an operetta I had done in Sydney for Opera Australia to perform on tour later that year. Life goes on, and no-one cares, really. Why should they? People are tied up in their own dramas, naturally. I do realise, however, how extraordinary it has been, this journey of a show that was never to be. And I like to think it would have been wonderful and that I would have brought something special to this iconic role.

I have those recordings of 'Everything's Coming up Roses' and 'Rose's Turn', which are now included on my three-CD set in the series, Great Australian Voices for Désirée Records. Also, I own a huge poster from that first cancelled production. I have never had the heart to have it framed or to hang it in my study with all my other posters. There were three only produced at the time. I know that Bruce Pollack, publicist of the first cancelled season has one.

One day, when I am in my dotage, and in the retirement village, I will have my poster framed and hung. Maybe I'll give it pride of place in my living room for all to see.

There are always a few annoying people throughout a long career, who run into you and say things like, 'Oh, I loved you in such and such.' They never accept it when you say, 'No. That was someone else. You are mixing me up with someone else. I never did that show.'

'No. It was you!' They insist. As if you don't know the shows you did or didn't do. It is so irritating.

But when someone comes to the retirement village to visit, probably an old theatre queen, and notices my fabulous poster of *Gypsy* up on my wall and says, 'God, you were great in that. Loved you in it. It was one of the best things you've ever done!'

You know what?

I won't deny it.

13

Moments in the Woods

*I*t is 1993. We are in production week of Into the Woods, *the Australian premiere, for the Sydney Theatre Company at the Drama Theatre at the Sydney Opera House. It is directed by Wayne Harrison and choreographed by Tony Bartuccio.*

I still sit on the Board of the company. STC has always had an actor on the Board. I am, therefore, wearing two hats, as I am also playing The Baker's Wife.

This is the worst production week in my entire career.

I think they allocate a couple of days technical rehearsal, followed by dress rehearsals, a couple of previews and opening night.

A week or more in, we are still doing the tech because of problems with the set and I call the chairman of the Board and tell him to get down to the Drama Theatre. I am wearing my Board hat. I remember saying to Wayne down the track, that if it had been any other director, he would have replaced that director.

I emphasise at this point that this season ended up being a huge hit, a sellout, and the set looked extraordinary. So, hats off to all the production team, particularly Wayne Harrison.

What happens is we end up postponing the opening for ten days. The set is quite complex. It consists of two huge raised circular playing areas, one inside the other, with a gap in the centre of the smaller circle. They both revolve either way and change heights independently, thereby creating different landscapes, playing areas, etc. The problem is that, if a character had to, say, crawl under the two revolves to enter from the middle gap section, he or she could be cut in half, literally. No safety measures are put into place in advance. It is an incredibly tense time as some cast members refuse to go on unless there is someone placed under the revolves at all times, with some signal to give to the actors that it is safe to proceed. It turns out to be a red light, green light system.

The day I have a screaming match with Wayne from the stage, ending with me walking off and slamming my dressing room door – something I regret almost immediately; actually I regret it as I am doing it – is the day Philip Quast's leg gets cut (not badly, thankfully) after slipping through the small gap between the circular revolves.

I should not have started the argument, certainly not publicly like that. I take full responsibility for my part in it. Tempers are frayed and the tension on stage is palpable. Wayne and I go back a long way, way back to No, No, Nanette, and have been close friends for years. This is just an argument over a play during a production week, when emotions are unusually high. Things are off the rails in this case. All will be fine between us, surely.

I do not hold grudges. I never have. Once things are said and are out in the open, it is over for me and I move on. I have had screaming matches with my mother my whole life. I forget, however, that some people do hold grudges ... forever.

On our opening night, Wayne gives me the Bette Davis book, No Guts, No Glory, in which he writes, 'Love Wayne'. I see that as a sign that all will be well. Not so. Things are never the same.

The first day of rehearsals for Into the Woods was interesting, to say the least. It was a stellar cast, a cast rich with big, opinionated actors who were not afraid to speak their minds. So when Wayne talked about his idea for the production containing a metaphor for all the people we lost from AIDS in the decade before, it did not go down well.

I guess an actor's job is to honour the writers and the script, while following the director's vision of a piece. But there was a lively discussion about Sondheim's intent for the show, particularly when our director wanted to set up a series of phone calls about arranging funerals to be prerecorded by the cast and played as the houselights faded before the start of the show. That idea stayed. As did the idea of the narrator character being a composer, perhaps Sondheim, sitting at a piano, with a New York skyline behind him and all of us circled around him at the piano as he created our stories. This was a step too far for some of us. I think that, if there are references to AIDS in the show, they are certainly oblique references. I believe audiences should take what they wish from all the things that happen in the woods, the consequences of some of the characters' actions. In my view, extra themes do not need to be spelled out. Still, I was an employed actor. I was not the director. So for once, I shut my mouth.

Anyway, it was not a good start. I recall one actor saying that day, 'I was hired to do *Into the Woods*, not this.'

However, we pushed on, as you do, and the show shaped up to be a wonderful piece of theatre, because of the team, the director, designer, lighting designer and choreographer. I include all of the actors in that as it was acted and sung incredibly well and audiences lapped it up.

We hit production week and fell into some sort of alternate universe. There was a strange, strange vibe. Apart from my falling out with the director, one of the major characters couldn't cope with all the angst of this extraordinary production week and didn't turn up for three days. I suspect there was alcohol involved. Two of the other actors had a punch-up in the corridor outside the Drama Theatre dressing rooms. It was quite awful, actually. The fight had to be broken up. Another actor swore she saw the ghost of Bennelong under the 'revolve'. She said that Bennelong did not want us to be performing *Into the Woods* at the Opera House and that was why there was so much strangeness in the air. Madness!

So she and a few others got in a spiritual healer to walk all over the set, under it, and around it, and bless each part of the construction. We were all invited to the blessing so that the gremlins could be placated and so that we could all be healed. Think I stayed in my dressing room for that one.

We opened to great success. Judi Connelli, who played the Witch, and Sharon Millerchip, Red Riding Hood, deservedly both won awards for their roles. It turned out to be a rich production, although it was decided that we should play it with Australian accents. I think the timing of the comedy is written for the American idiom, so that aspect did not sit well with me. Still, we made it work and we were a hit. Thank God. Otherwise we might have killed each other.

We closed. I was still on the Board, although Wayne ignored me at all meetings. He was trying to freeze me off the Board by treating me with disdain at every meeting. It was difficult for me emotionally, to keep turning up to meetings. You could've cut the air with a knife. Not one Board member came to my rescue. They fence sat. I believe to this day, that they all treated me shabbily, as if it had been my fault that the show had missed its opening night and lost some revenue because of it. Several of my friends kept saying that I should not let Wayne win by resigning. I didn't see it that way. Win? Lose? Rubbish! It wasn't about that. I kept hoping for some sort of reconciliation between Wayne and me.

Things continued to be very tricky.

At one stage, Wayne and I were called in to a mediation to try to sort out our differences. It didn't go too well.

I said how impossible it was for me, being on the Board, wearing two hats at once, watching things fall apart in that production week, and being an actor in the show. I went on to apologise again for my outburst. I regretted it deeply and regretted that the argument had caused such a rift in our friendship. It was wrong of me and I owned my part in it.

I had no positive response from Wayne, in fact no response at all. It was evident he was not going to give an inch. I remember saying, 'The ship was sinking. I was on the Board. What was I supposed to do?' And Wayne replying, 'You were my friend. You should have been prepared to go down in the ship with me.'

There was no coming back from that. I am sure in Wayne's world, an alternative perspective exists. I have no doubt the whole incident will appear in his book one day with an entirely different version. Our recollections are always informed by our own personal hurts. They alter, sometimes distort over time.

Just before I did *Into the Woods*, I did a series of concerts in Zimbabwe, with

Greg Crease as my MD. We had put together a quite sophisticated show, full of Coward, Porter and Gershwin. We were playing in Harare in a wonderful hotel. It was a job for Qantas, with an all-expenses-paid safari thrown into the deal. Boy, did we misread the audience in Africa. Allow me to paint the picture for you. They would have preferred an Elvis impersonator.

Our concerts were excruciating, trying to play sophisticated material, with no lights on the platform stage that had been erected for me, and a buffet right next to us. So, not only was there no focus on the performance area, with the lack of light, but also folk constantly walked back and forth in front of me to grab food, while I was singing, talking all the while. Every night, Greg Crease and I would eat dinner together in our adjoining suites, and then take the long slow walk towards another 'death' in the performance room. Every time I see Greg, we say, 'We'll always have Africa.'

Just before we left Harare, we went to a local market and I talked to a witch doctor. He sold me 'true love and happiness'. It took the form of a few nutshells and seeds. He said to carry them in my wallet and I would discover love. I laughed, as did he, as I handed over money to him for the shells and seeds, both of us not believing for a second, that true love would come from these few ordinary shells and seeds; that he was pulling the wool over my eyes. Still, I carried those seeds and shells in my wallet.

A few months later, I met Brian.

14

Never Too Late for Love

I have a series of Broadway concerts coming up at the then Lyric Opera of Queensland (now Opera Queensland) to be conducted by Brian Castles-Onion, whom my friend I have known since school, Milton Griffin, tells me I will really like. I speak to Brian quite a lot about repertoire for the concert, before meeting him in person. I like him even then. Mother would have said, 'I like the sound of him.'

When I first see Brian, he runs down the stairs of the Lyric Opera rehearsal rooms and kisses me on the cheek. He tells me later he never does that. People say that when you meet the right person, you just know. I just know. So does he.

Brian and I are engaged within two weeks of meeting. My Sydney friends think I have gone mad. My favourite film is Frank Capra's It's a Wonderful Life. Brian has never seen it. I make him watch it and threaten jokingly that if he doesn't cry at least three times, I won't marry him. He does cry, more than three times, so he passes the marriage audition with flying colours.

We didn't marry until five months later, on New Year's Eve. I had always hated New Year's Eve, the expectation of it all. And I remember my mother spoiling many of them by causing huge rows so that I wouldn't enjoy going out. She was jealous of me having friends. She did this over and over throughout the years. Mother loves wearing the destroyer hat. It is her favourite role to play.

Naturally, I look forward to something to celebrate on New Year's Eve.

∽

What a great and happy surprise it was to meet Brian. I thought I would never have a partner again. He asked me to marry him and my friends thought I'd lost my mind, I was visiting him in Brisbane not long after. He was still head of music there, before he moved to Sydney and back to Opera Australia. I decided I would like to visit my parents' graves. I had never been back. Of course, my brother Noel was buried there as well.

Brian drove me. It was before the computerisation of cemeteries, so you had to look around for the graves. I remembered that I had been happy at the time that Mum had been buried close to a rather busy road, so I knew, vaguely, the place to search. I was comforted at the time by the fact that she would have all that bustle and life going on around her. She'd like that.

Brian found the graves. As I walked towards them, he stepped back to allow me some privacy. It was upsetting. Lots of memories flooded back as I stood there, with tears slowly rolling down my cheeks. I was there for quite a while. Finally, I walked towards where Brian was standing. He said quietly, 'I feel as if I've met them.'

I thought, 'Yes. I'll marry you.'

It was the kindness in him, you see. For many years, when he was conducting, he kept a swatch of fabric from my wedding dress stuffed into the inside pocket of his tailcoat, next to his heart.

The next week I returned to Sydney and resigned from the Board of Sydney Theatre Company. I was looking to the future. I had no need for that shit any longer.

The final insult, apart from being removed from the invitation lists of the Sydney Theatre Company from that day on, something enjoyed by all former Board members, was that I never received a reply accepting my resignation from the Chairman. I should've thought such a letter was obligatory. No. Not even a form letter thanking me for my service. Zip. It was rude. I should've kept turning up to meetings until I received a formal reply!

In between our engagement and the marriage, the saga of *Sunset Boulevard* continued. I had been expected for the last couple of years, to play Norma Desmond in Australia. I had worked with the musical director in charge of the show while he had been in Australia. He had been extremely complimentary and the Australian team expected that it would become a done deal. Overtures were made. I recorded 'As If We Never Said Goodbye' for the management, to be released as a single down the track for publicity purposes. Huge floral tributes were sent to me from the management as congratulations for the recording. They seemed excited at the prospect of me playing this role. I believed the management was serious, although no formal offer had been forthcoming.

I had not met with Andrew Lloyd Webber and Trevor Nunn for the obligatory final audition. During the second half of 1993, Brian came to Sydney for a weekend visit. He was still with Lyric Opera in Queensland. I was suddenly called to fly to LA for my meeting with Trevor and Andrew that weekend. Julie Brooks was sent with me as my chaperone. It was a little overwhelming. I have never been good at flying long distances and singing. I usually need a few days to recover from the flight. However, I was flown up the front of the plane and stayed in one of those lovely cottages at Hotel Bel Air. The management looked after me well.

The audition came and went. I didn't think I sang as well as I usually sing. I was nervous. Andrew paced up and down at the back of the theatre in an unengaged way, while Trevor worked with me on stage.

After I returned to Australia to see Brian, things went very quiet about the show and about the possibility of me being cast. This coincided with Patti LuPone parting ways with the show in London. Perhaps they thought I was the equivalent of Miss LuPone in Australia and therefore they went cold on the prospect of casting me. All I remember is the management stopped returning calls from my representatives. This was not a good sign. If it were good news, surely I would have heard straight away. Months went by. Finally, I received a message.

Word for word: 'Trevor knows within five minutes of meeting someone if he wants to work with them. He knew within five minutes, he didn't want to work with you.'

As I said in an interview in 2019, 'What the fuck is that???'

Now, perhaps this was something my management at the time made up to let me down gently. News flash, it didn't. Perhaps it was something one of their management's assistants came up with in that moment. I can but hope that this had not really come from Trevor Nunn.

Anyway, the rest is history. Some things are meant to be and some are not.

Brian moved down to Sydney a couple of months before our marriage. I was rehearsing the reopening of the newly renovated Civic Theatre in Newcastle, with a show called *A Rare Jewel,* an original play, with a jukebox score. That's a story in itself, as the producers hadn't thought to get the rights from the composers. We almost didn't open. Much drama!

During rehearsals, Brian arrived at the Petersham house in Sydney, where we were to marry, before coming up to Newcastle to join me for the opening. The day he arrived in Sydney, coincided with me suffering a migraine and staying home from rehearsals in Newcastle. For a few years I had suffered the odd migraine, where the result was I threw up for twenty-four hours. Thankfully, they have since disappeared.

On my sick bed, I received a call from Brian saying that on his arrival, obviously there had been a break in, as parts of the house had been trashed, and the police wanted to talk to me about making an inventory about exactly what had been taken.

I hopped in the car and drove down to Sydney, stopping about four times to throw up along the way. The last time was on the Harbour Bridge, in the centre lane. There was nowhere to pull over. I had no choice. I threw up all over myself, bursting into tears at the same time. I kept driving. I turned up at the house to greet my future husband, looking an absolute picture and smelling of roses!

It turned out the police knew the thief, a young drag queen. He had mistakenly left his diary in my study, along with his one-day pass from a juvenile detention centre. I wondered why all my sparkly paste jewellery I used for concerts had been stolen, along with all my show records and my Longchamp luggage. All my real jewels had been scattered on the floor and left behind, luckily. Guess they didn't have enough bling. With all the posters of my shows in my study, I can only imagine the excitement when this young drag queen realised whose house he had broken into.

Brian and I were married on New Year's Eve, with many wonderful friends present. I had a big tax debt when I met Brian. I had bought Greg out of the 'Consulate' in Petersham, had a mortgage I couldn't climb over, and had fallen behind with my tax obligations. The house had to go to pay the debt. Brian had won a Churchill Fellowship to study conducting in Italy so I sold the house, paid the debt and we started again, with a little cottage in south Newtown, and travelled overseas on an extended honeymoon. Brian studied.

Our best time was had in Venice, where we met with one of Brian's mentors, Randy Mickelson. We visited his palazzo every day, all day, a famous palazzo, on the fashionable bend of the Grand Canal, where vaporetti passed by on a regular basis, and I often found myself waving to tourists from the terrace as they floated past. They pointed and waved, imagining I was a rich Venetian. Brian and Randy talked and talked and listened to great singers. Randy would make lunch or we'd go to one of his many favourite eateries, like Harry's Bar. It felt like we were really living the dream.

It was an old fashioned teaching experience, in which you spent all day with the teacher, soaking in everything he spoke of, sometimes arguing, sometimes meeting classical singers, all the while drinking in the glory that is Venice. It was fabulous.

I returned home after our European jaunt and our trip to New York to see some shows. Brian came back home at a later date, to see his father, who was ill, and stayed on for his father's funeral. Then Brian returned to Europe to continue to fulfil his fellowship obligations. Brian's father, who had been a miner in Cessnock all his life, had been 'dusted', as they called it, and had suffered from ill health for some years. Brian was born on his father's birthday and Brian's father died on my birthday.

I had longed for a child for years. It seemed it was too late for me, by the time I met Brian. However, you find a way to cope as the years go by. Our dogs have always been our children. I have a godson, Henry, who is the son of my very good friend, Pleasance Ingle, who used to be wardrobe mistress at Her Majesty's Theatre in Sydney. She was my dresser on many shows and we became close friends. In fact, she was my bridesmaid when I married Brian and her daughter, Isabella, now with a daughter of her own, was my flower girl. Our friend, Milton Griffin was best man. For our wedding, the house was decorated by designer, Roger Kirk. Linda Nagle did the flowers, which were extraordinary. The house looked so wonderful, overflowing with flowers, the famous Sydney Theatre Company candelabras everywhere, and our friends singing and playing.

I walked in to Gershwin's 'Love Walked In', played by Max Lambert. Peter Carroll and Diane Smith, who had played a wonderful Charlotte in the STC's *A Little Night Music,* performed readings: Peter, a Shakespearean sonnet and Di, a wonderful passage from *The Velveteen Rabbit,* one of my favourite books.

There was much music, much singing and eating and drinking. It was a marvellous night. Philip Quast has still not given us his gift. Every time I see him, he says he must get it to us. It is apparently in his attic.

In 1994, I was playing Lalume for several performances in a concert version of *Kismet* in Melbourne for Victoria State Opera. What an absolutely gorgeous score! Brian didn't see it, as he was overseas at the time. He returned from all his studies and went back to work at Opera Australia.

I was offered a one-off job for the NSW Racing Industry Association at a swanky hotel in Sydney around this time. I was to sing at a dinner, with Greg Crease as MD. I should have thought the better of it as I hate anything to do with horse racing, the cruelty of it all. We arrived for the sound check. The vast room was decorated beautifully, flowers dripping off columns, candelabra everywhere. The organiser walked out to greet us and gave us the key to a posh suite where we could go until the concert, with all drinks and food included.

I happened to say, 'Where is the piano?'

His face went ashen; all colour drained from him.

'There's no piano,' he said, almost in the broken voice of a teenage boy.

'Well. You'd better find one,' I said, as Greg and I headed for the elevator.

Some time later, the phone rang in our suite. I answered. The male voice said, 'Could I talk to the man?'

I didn't even go there. I handed the phone to Greg without speaking. Greg kept saying, 'Hmm, hmm, hmm.'

He hung up. Told me they had found a keyboard of sorts that they could borrow from a band playing at another function in the hotel. Greg agreed to go down to look at it. He came back and said that we were going home. It was not a full keyboard and had no sustain pedal.

We left. They refused to pay us. We had turned up in good faith to do a job and there had been a huge oversight, a mistake of the organiser, not us. I wrote a letter explaining that it was the equivalent of having thoroughbred racehorses replaced by donkeys for a major race (with apologies to donkeys – I love donkeys!).

Since that time, I always state that my list of requirements must include a piano. Seems you must state the obvious.

Brian and I eventually sold our little cottage in Newtown and bought a bigger house, with a driveway and parking, really sought after in the inner city, just up the road in Enmore.

We renovated it, lived there for a few years before selling and moving to the Southern Highlands, where commuting remains a part of our lives. I don't mind the driving. I pop on the radio or a podcast and I'm home before I know it. Brian hates the commute. It is worth it to live in such a beautiful place. The payoff is the peace and beauty, a large garden brimming with roses, my mother's favourites, a great community, no humidity like Sydney, and four distinct seasons, so good for the soul.

Brian's mother was Scottish and Brian has red hair. If I were to believe that my mother's 'guide' in the afterlife is a Scottish laird, with long red hair, wearing a kilt, it is not a huge leap to make a connection.

Is it wishful thinking to believe my mother might have liked Brian?

15

There is Beauty in the Bellow of the Blast

*I*t is 1995. I am performing Katisha in Mikado for the last time. We are more than *halfway through a Melbourne season at Her Majesty's Theatre after seasons in Brisbane, Sydney and Newcastle.*

There is a problem with a proposal of a DVD of the production. I misread the mood of the cast and try to fight, with my usual zest for activism, for a larger payment for everyone. It turns out the cast are happy to simply appear on a DVD. They don't care much about the money. I obviously upset the management, by not giving up on this issue.

There is a loophole in my contract, an 'out' clause for me and for the producer, which has been set up from the outset. The producer gets rid of me through that loophole, immediately takes leave to avoid any possible awkwardness (he is also in the show), and flies in my replacement to stand in the wings watching, while I play out my two weeks notice.

My management lies to me and tells me that the show is closing but I mustn't tell anyone. To what end, I have no idea. As if I won't find out I am being replaced? How ridiculous! Not long after, I notice the future Katisha watching me perform from the wings.

I part with that management because of this total fuck up.

So, I am playing my last show. You've got to love show folk. After my final exit, the cast is standing in the wings applauding me, as I exit and my eyes well up.

❧

I said 'yes' to this show instead of saying 'yes' to Wayne Harrison for a production of *Who's Afraid of Virginia Woolf*. I needed the commercial theatre income at the time, but I would have loved to play Martha; a great role for me. I regret that. That was the last time Wayne ever offered me a part.

With this production of *Mikado*, everything felt uneasy from the get-go. I was told many times and in many ways that I was not to make waves during the season. I didn't understand this, as I had been friendly with the producer over the years and anyway, what did that mean? If they felt I was going to be a problem, then why offer me the role? Did my reputation about trashing Greg Jones's office (which never happened) precede me? Or was it the drama that took place during *Into the Woods*? I have no idea. All I know is that I am a very reasonable person and a fiercely loyal colleague. This narrative was totally unwarranted.

Still, we proceeded with the contract, hoping everything would settle down, and rehearsals turned out to be delightful. Jon English's role had been built up so that he was the outright lead. Drew Forsythe played Ko-Ko and we got on incredibly well, working together for the first time. All the reviews praised the show, and me. I believe the part of Katisha was a good fit for me.

What was my reaction to being erased from a production? I was devastated. It took me a long, long time to live through it. I say, 'live through', as I believe you don't get over anything really. Everything that happens becomes a part of who you are and you learn to live with it. It is similar to the grief you feel when you lose someone. Over the years, you absorb it into your body and go on each day with the knowledge that person lives within you.

Throughout my life, I have thought many times that I am over something until I run into that person who 'done me wrong' or someone brings up something in a conversation, by chance about an incident that had hurt years before, and my stomach immediately knots and drops from under me.

My conclusion is that everything that happens to us lives inside us, forever. Every life is made up of all this muscle memory. There is no point trying to get through to the other side.

I sense that some people, who don't know me very well at all, and I do stress that, have continued to misjudge me throughout my life. Am I partly to blame for that? Is my demeanour scary or guarded or something? Is my poker face just too good? The number of times I have worked with someone for the first time, and that person says at the end of a couple of weeks rehearsing, 'You're really lovely,' in a surprised tone.

This 'difficult' reputation has followed me around unfairly. Things are changing as I age. I suppose young performers know nothing of my past anyway, or simply can't imagine that an older woman is capable of making waves. Perhaps people think I have mellowed. Don't think so. Don't intend to.

I am opinionated and outspoken and will continue to be until my last breath. I used to dislike it about myself, not that I can change who I am. I have come to realise that it is one of my best qualities. I cannot stand fence-sitters, people who say nothing at times when they should speak up.

I hate injustice. I am at my best when my back is against the wall. It is then that I come out fighting. I love a good fight. My family always sat around the kitchen table shouting at each other. I suppose some families are much more gentle. Indeed, some people mistakenly believe I am tough, or ruthless, or cutthroat or words like that. Nothing could be further from the truth. What you see is not what you get with people. You must look beneath the surface.

The truth is I am marshmallow. I am insecure. I am easily hurt. But I do possess bluster and resilience. These things I inherited, I have no doubt, from my mother.

I remember talking to a therapist once about feeling overwhelmed and so despairing at certain times in my life, that I can sink to the floor and stay there wishing my life would end. 'But I have never stayed on the floor for long. I get bored with myself, snap out of it, get up, put the kettle on and have a cup of tea.'

When the therapist said, 'Geraldine, some people never get up from the floor,' I was shocked.

'Really? They don't?'

I had to think about that and came to the conclusion that I am a tenacious girl. However, I do not deal with rejection very well at all. Rejection is something an actor has to get used to and find the confidence to toss off, and that takes some practice. I have never been able to do it. Mind you, the greatest performers all possess a fine balance of ego and vulnerability. I loathe performances where an actor wears his or her ego in front of them. That, I find ghastly.

I have lost my temper no more than five times in a more than fifty-year career, and most of the time, the reasons were absolutely warranted. If I were a man, I would have been lauded for caring so much about my craft that I would go to such lengths. Being a woman, the word 'hysterical' is bandied about and words that do not even exist to describe men, words like 'bitch' are thrown out. I can only hope things are changing. With feminism, it is often two steps forward, one step back. We have a long way to go.

Not long before doing *Mikado*, Terry Ashton-Wood called me one night about 3 am and woke both Brian and me. I had known him for years. He had produced the first Sondheim concert I had ever taken part in, an AIDS benefit at the Independent Theatre in North Sydney some years before. I recall Sondheim had donated all his royalties to the cause at the time.

Terry had lived for years, on and off, with the divine Colleen Clifford, Sydney theatre identity, singing teacher, pianist and performer. She had appeared in the film *Careful, He Might Hear You*, the only time I had ever worked with her. Who knows how old she really was. Colleen was ancient, I fear, tiny and glamorous. I had met her when I had moved to Sydney years before, as she was my first husband's singing teacher.

For years, she was at every theatre opening, encouraging everyone and staying up later than most people who were at least forty years her junior. Colleen used to do one-woman shows, sitting at a piano, singing, telling stories. Often, she would fall asleep in the middle of her show – just for a few seconds. Audiences patiently waited until Colleen woke up with a start, realised where she was and went on with her show.

She also used to play certain notes on the piano with her foot. She would suddenly kick her leg and land it on the keys, with a perfect chord being played with her heel. You know already my long-held appreciation of sight acts. This fell into that category so well.

I can't remember ever seeing Colleen without false eyelashes or a fully made-up face. Dear Colleen 'exited the stage', as they say, in 1996.

She had looked after Terry, and he, her, for some years until he eventually moved out on his own. Terry was a theatrical agent for some time, I remember.

At the time of this call from Terry, Brian and I had not been married all that long. Terry was living in a small public housing flat in The Rocks in Sydney and had fallen on hard times, workwise. Terry called in the middle of the night, said he was depressed and pleaded with me to come over.

If the truth were known, he had probably gone through his friends' list and everyone else had hung up on him. He had reached the 'Ts' in his phone book. Suddenly, Brian and I were in the car, driving to his place, as I thought he might be in some sort of trouble. Instinctively, I knew that he was in need, in need of a friend. I was not going to be the person who rejected him or turned a blind eye to his plight.

On arrival, we realised he had been drinking all night or had taken something, or both, as he could hardly stand up when he let us in. After much cajoling, he agreed to get into bed. Brian, bless him, helped me take his shoes off and pull the covers up.

This is how the conversation went.

Me: 'Now try to go to sleep.'

Terry: 'Sing some Sondheim to me.'

Me: 'What?'

Terry: 'I'll try to go to sleep if you sing me some Sondheim. Will you wait till I fall asleep?'

Me: 'Of course.'

There I was at four o'clock in the morning in a tiny apartment under the Sydney Harbour Bridge, working my way through my repertoire of Sondheim songs, trying not to sing so loudly that the entire building would complain, while the drunken, drug fucked Terry kept applauding and squealing gleefully, 'Just one more, please.'

I can't remember how many songs I sang. It was exhausting. Eventually, he dropped off to sleep. We tip-toed out and drove home. The sun was well and truly up. I was in track pants with no makeup, looking two hundred and feeling wretched. Terry was absolutely fine.

Hi, ho, the glamorous life.

16

Once in a Blue Moon

The lyrics of the musical, **Summer Rain** *represent Australian writer, Nick Enright at his best. The book is also by Nick and the musical score by Terence Clarke. I play Ruby for Robyn Nevin at the Queensland Theatre Company in her opening season as artistic director.*

It is a fantastic show, set in 1930s rural Australia about a troupe of travelling tent show players arriving in a small town and the consequences that occur. Nick interpolates some fantastic 'Australianisms' of the period into some of the lyrics. It is a perfect choice for the opening of a new season, as the play reminds us, as we follow this troupe of players and town folk, why we are performers and why we keep on doing it; why we persist in carrying on in the business when times are really tough, and the absolute elation of a hit show and an audience held in rapture. Harold (Bille Brown), and Ruby sing the wonderful song, 'Once In a Blue Moon' near the beginning of Act Two.

Apart from acting with Ms Nevin on several occasions on stage and screen, I have worked twice with Robyn directing me and both times have been fantastic experiences.

In 1996, Robyn asked me to play Pearl in a tour for the Melbourne Theatre Company of *The Summer of the Seventeenth Doll*. Pearl is a role I had always wanted to play. I believe it to be one of the best things I have done. Ray Lawler, the writer of this classic, came to see the production in Adelaide and loved our production. Robyn did a fabulous job of directing it. We also played the three-tiered Georgian marvel that is the Theatre Royal in Hobart, the oldest theatre in Australia. This tour, surrounded by a fantastic company and being blessed with the privilege of performing this show each night, was the happiest tour I had been a part of in years. I think I laughed every day. Well, you do when Lois Ramsay, Nadine Garner and Genevieve Lemon are in the cast. We were all good. So were the boys, the divine Peter Curtin and the fabulous Neil Melville. It is such a well-constructed play and an absolute delight to be a part of.

Ms Nevin became the artistic director of the Queensland Theatre Company the following year and asked me to play in the wonderful Australian musical *Summer Rain* to open her season. Working at QTC always felt like coming home. Nick Enright was there for rehearsals to tweak the script. This show had originally been written for drama students then it had been rewritten and rewritten, for Sydney Theatre Company and other companies. There had been several iterations of the piece. Actually, my cousin Caz's son, Sandro Colarelli, was in this cast. It was great to work together on this fabulous piece.

During our rehearsals, runs of a large section of Act Two did not seem to flow. I stayed up one night and took it upon myself to rearrange some scenes, sent off my ideas to Robyn and waited for the 'Why don't you keep out of it?' speech from her the next day. Instead, she surprised me and said that we would rehearse Geraldine's version of the sequence of these scenes. It worked, and they stayed in that order! I did feel quite chuffed about that, but even more so, when Nick and Terry wrote a new song for me, 'Abracadabra Man', which remains in the show to this day. Recently, while cleaning out my study, I found a lovely card from Terry Clarke, where he talks about always wanting to write a show for me, but that this song, which they wrote especially for me, would have to do for now. That is special. Ruby sings 'Abracadabra Man', a wonderful ballad, early in Act Two, about her husband, Harold.

The other time a song was written especially for me happened years later, in 2005, when I appeared in the show that reopened The Q Theatre in Penrith: a show called *Somewhere* by Tim Minchin and Kate Mulvany, early in both their writing careers.

My character was a wicked witch type of woman, called Philomena, with the play, within a play, containing many allusions to *The Wizard of Oz*. I had some terrific songs written by Tim, but they were all up-tempo, and specific to the action, but not to her. I was chatting to Tim Minchin one day during a coffee break and suggested that it might be great to have a ballad for Philomena in Act Two, which is an inner monologue, where she reveals to the audience that she has never learned how to show affection, or kindness. But it is within her to do so.

He liked the idea. While we continued to rehearse, he went into another room. He emerged a couple of hours later, sat down and played and sang me the most beautiful song, 'So Much Love', which was interpolated into the show for me. It appears on my Great Australian Voices three-CD set for Désirée Records, and is on an album of Tim's as a bonus track, in which he introduces the song by talking about writing it for me.

I returned home after rehearsals that day and said to Brian, 'That Tim Minchin is going somewhere.'

In the beginning of 1997, I was in Brisbane doing some concerts, when I received the awful news that my cousin Susan's daughter, her only child, had been killed, along with her boyfriend, in an horrific car accident. Naturally, I attended the funeral and burial at the Gold Coast, with my cousin, Caz. The church was overflowing. After all, they were teenagers, so many school friends were there. It was awful.

We were at the burial. I stress I mean no disrespect or disparagement of poor Susan, who was palpably grief- stricken from an unthinkable loss of her only child. In a surreal moment, as the final prayer was being spoken and the coffin lowered into the ground, Susan leapt into the grave in hysteria. Some men took charge and got her out. The rest of us stood frozen, not saying anything, not looking at anything in particular.

I had never experienced anything like it. Perhaps it happens more than you would imagine. I say that because of what the priest did. He didn't seem surprised. He placed his arm gently around Susan and walked her, as she continued to sob, away from all of us, quite a long way away. Time stood still. No-one spoke.

Eventually, they returned. The priest simply said, 'We'll start the prayer again.' The coffin was lowered. The service ended.

I thought it was very classy of him to handle this situation so well. As I was standing there in that moment when time blurred, I did think that if you wrote this in a script, would people believe it?

Then I thought, this is my family, so none of this is at all surprising.

In 1997 I also worked for the first time for Australian producer John Frost. I had first met John when he worked for a time for Bill Shanahan as an agent many years earlier. That role ended up not suiting him and he began a production company with Ashley Gordon, whom we lost at a very early age during that dreadful decade, the eighties, when AIDS ravaged our community.

In any case, I had heard that Richard Wherrett was directing a new production of *Cabaret* at the Footbridge Theatre in Sydney. I took Richard to lunch to try to talk him into casting me as Fräulein Schneider. I had seen a few productions of the stage version and had longed, for some years, to play this fabulous role, which had been created originally, for the great Lotte Lenya. Richard was reluctant to cast me as he thought I was too young and too beautiful, his words.

I talked him around, a few glasses of wine later. The reason he succumbed to my suggestion was that he said that when an actor is so intent on playing a role, and goes to great lengths to talk the director into it, there is usually a great outcome. Happily, I was cast.

Ross Coleman choreographed and Roger Kirk designed. The winning team from *Chicago* was together again. Angela Toohey played Sally. She was so like Liza Minnelli in her interpretation that it worked for audiences.

I think that the film of *Cabaret* and Liza's portrayal in it has made it almost impossible to present the stage show as it was intended originally. Audiences expect Liza. Liza is amazing as Sally Bowles; it is a star turn. However, I believe the tragedy of the piece really is that audiences should know that

Sally is never going to make it. Therefore, her giving up everything, including her pregnancy, to follow her dream becomes all the more poignant. It is a fine line to tread in a musical; that is, to act being a mediocre performer, while being good enough to sing and dance in a satisfying way to please an audience. That takes real talent.

Judi Dench managed it brilliantly – a British girl, out of her depth, pretending to lead what she perceives as a sophisticated life. Julie Harris in *I Am a Camera*, the original non-musical film version of the story, is also wonderful as Sally.

Ross, of course, did an exemplary job of choreographing our production. It was a marriage made in heaven: Ross Coleman and *Cabaret*. Ross was a master at choreographing sexually suggestive numbers that never went too far to become vulgar.

The season was a success and we ran a number of weeks.

My brother Ralph died during that season. My brother Leigh called me with the news. He didn't say, 'Ralph. Dead.'

I flew up to the Sunshine Coast on my day off, for his funeral. Ralph's wife, Jewel, asked if I would like to see him and I felt I had to go into the viewing room. So, my cousin Coralie said that she would come in with me. As I entered the room and saw Ralph in his coffin in a shroud, my mind raced back to all those arguments, all that resentment over my becoming an actress and not, in his view, using the education he had paid for.

I had not seen him in a long time. Mum, Dad, and Noel had all dropped dead of heart attacks, as had Ralph. There he was, lying there, somewhat unrecognisable, with a trickle of what looked like perspiration on his forehead. That was weird. I thought for a split second that he was still alive. It was condensation, I suspect.

I felt nothing. I really didn't know him at all. In fact, if I had been left alone in a room with him over the years prior to this, I would not have known what to say. There was a stranger lying in that coffin, a stranger who was my brother.

Leigh was still in Perth, where he continues to reside, so didn't manage to get to the funeral. I returned the next day to Sydney, to the start of another week of the show. I didn't miss a performance.

Mum had a favourite son in her first born, Ralph. The other boys knew it. I knew that I had meant more to her than all of my brothers. The boys knew that too. Perhaps they had been jealous of that. Really, though, it had been a curse to be her chosen one, the one expected to live her life for her. I had never truly been able to escape her tight hold over me, nor had I been successful enough for her. It was an impossible task to please her, to be enough of anything for her.

As I flew back to perform again in *Cabaret*, an overwhelming sense of sadness came over me. And I thought again that no happiness had ever come from our family.

17

Loose Ends

It is August 2002 and it is the opening night of The Witches of Eastwick, at the Princess Theatre in Melbourne. I am playing Felicia Gabriel. But I am not there.

This is the only opening night I have ever missed in my entire career. In fact, I am not one to miss performances at all.

I catch a bad cold during the last week of rehearsals. It doesn't go away. We move to the theatre for a couple of weeks of previews, changing the script each night, changes shoved under our dressing room doors at times, with handwritten notes from the writers, John Dempsey and Dana P. Rowe that read, 'Say this tomorrow night in such and such a scene.'

I remain unwell. In fact, my dresser and my wig person (I change wigs for every scene, each one a different colour) are actually holding me up while doing my costume changes as I have difficulty remaining in an upright position. I am so sick, but my strong will keeps me fighting on. Finally, my dresser goes to stage management after the show one night and suggests that this situation cannot go on.

Cameron Macintosh and Rodney Rigby, the Australian producer, give me some days off to recover. By now, my voice is strained from the pushing I am doing just to get through the shows. I am given a deadline by the management to get well. Understandably, they are worried for their upcoming opening. But as soon as you say to someone who is fighting an illness, you must be well by, say, Friday, you are *never going to be well by that given day. The pressure is too much. I do the show on the given day, but I am not well still. I am called in to the office and told that I am not doing the opening. I am to go back to Sydney for a couple of weeks, under a doctor's supervision, and then return to the show. I do that. My doctor diagnoses pneumonia. No wonder I am so unwell.*

However, once I give in to being ill, accept it, rather than keep fighting all the time to get well, things start to improve. I start major drug treatment and am back to the show two weeks later.

My old friend John Robertson is very sympathetic on the night they tell me I am not doing the opening. Obviously, I am devastated. I do 'humping crying' as they tell me to go home to Sydney and get well. They end up flying out Rosemary Ashe, who had done the London production, to take over in my absence.

I am happily surprised and touched to see Cameron Macintosh turn up to my apartment the next morning and carry my suitcases to the limo he supplies to get me to the airport. He is very kind to me. He talks of coming back for the Sydney opening to see me in the role and celebrate with me. I am touched at his generosity. Not since Oliver! in 1984, have I had anything to do with Cameron.

But there is no Sydney opening.

We close sixteen weeks later.

❧

Back in the late nineties, I had toured in *Grease: The Arena Spectacular*, for John Frost, followed by a musical revue of Kurt Weill songs, called *Simply Weill*, at the Sydney Opera House, for Stephen Helper, who also wrote and directed it. I imagined reviewers writing headlines like, 'Simply Weill … and it was!'

Nevertheless, it was a great season and the reviews were universally positive. It certainly deepened my love of this material. To this day, I include at least one Weill song in any concert. I love the fact that the feel of Weill's music changed almost completely; depending on which lyricist he was working with at the time and the fact that he had two separate and very different careers in Germany and the US.

After my one stint working for The Production Company in *Call Me Madam* in 2000, I returned to my old home of the Queensland Theatre Company to play one of the leads, opposite Bille Brown (who had played my husband in *Summer Rain*), in the Ostrovsky play, *The Forest*.

Robyn Nevin had wanted to play the role for the company when she had been artistic director, but it didn't eventuate. She then got the job of artistic director of the Sydney Theatre Company at the end of Wayne Harrison's tenure and recommended me for the role of Raisa in *The Forest*, as the play was still on the 'to do' list of the company.

It was a huge and exciting challenge for me, playing this gift of a role in a wonderful Russian play, reminiscent of a Chekhov piece.

I worked again, after many years, with Bryan Nason, who had run the College Players all those years before and had given me a chance, casting me in *Salad Days* when I was just out of school. He was a part of the marvellous cast. It was a terrific production and a very happy time in the theatre, playing at the Playhouse at the Queensland Performing Arts Centre.

I certainly recall the final night of this play. My great friend, Peter Eyers, who, as I have previously mentioned, produces a series of podcasts called *Stages*, which is turning into a rich history of Australian theatre, had flown up to Brisbane to see it and to drive back to Sydney with me the next day, dogs in tow. I had had a really friendly relationship with one of the younger members of the cast. I stress 'friendly' as absolutely no romance was a part of it. However, I guess there was some sort of innocent flirtatiousness between us under the surface. Enjoyable, light banter, that was it. In fact Brian teased me about it relentlessly.

Why then did I burst into tears at the last-night party? These were not regular tears. They came from somewhere deep inside me, some place of incredible loss. I had felt this unstoppable display of grief only once before. That was at a school reunion, when we all went to the chapel at school for a special service. I exited the chapel and the tears and almost prehistoric grunting noises from deep within me began.

A short time after the season of *The Forest*, I had dinner and a drink with friend Jacki Weaver and told her about that final night and the guttural sounds and uncontrollable crying, and my absolute disbelief that I could not control this feeling, this inexplicable emotion. She understood my sense of grief on a deep level. We agreed that it had come from a place of tremendous loss, the notion that age brings with it the almost unbearable disappointment that any sort of frisson that might have happened in a show when we had been young and dewy was well and truly a thing of the past.

I saw Alan Wylie, my former husband, while I was in Brisbane playing this role in *The Forest*. I received a message at the theatre that he was in town and had read that I was performing at QPAC. He didn't suggest that he was interested in seeing the play, which I found a little disappointing, but instead suggested we have a coffee between shows on the final Saturday. Peter Eyers came with me, just in case I felt the need to escape quickly. It was nice to see Alan after so many years. He was still living with our bridesmaid. Some things are meant to be. We had nothing much to talk about. As I watched him leave, I thought to myself that it had been the correct decision to end our marriage all those years ago. I have not seen or heard of him since. I do wish him well.

The season of *The Witches of Eastwick* limped to the end of the Melbourne run. It never really captured the public's imagination, although there were some great performances in the cast. Paul McDermott was fabulous in the leading role, as were Marina Prior, Angela Toohey and Pippa Grandison as the witches. Tony Sheldon played my husband, relishing the comedy in his role.

I never really relaxed during that season. It was odd to have missed my opening night. Because of that, I think I didn't trust that I would remain well. I rested more than I had ever rested during any run. I was cautious by day. I visited an acupuncturist and a masseur each week to keep me on track with my health.

What was fun for me was performing some magic tricks each night and signing the 'magic contract' to never reveal how the tricks were achieved. That felt very grown up.

As we soldiered on and on towards an eventual closing, hoping for a turnaround in audience numbers, Rodney Rigby asked all the principals if we would take a cut in our salaries. We had a meeting and decided that even if we agreed to that, the management could very well give us notice soon after anyway. It was decided to keep the status quo. A week later, the company got its notice and we closed three weeks after that.

It was a fun cast to work with and a fun show to do. I believe it has never really taken off as a musical because most of the characters are awful people. There is no-one particularly for the audience to root for. It is funny and clever. The score is terrific. It certainly moves fast. The characters are interesting, if unlikeable.

This version of the show was the version they were to take to New York. That is why we rehearsed so many changes during the previews. The transfer to Broadway didn't happen. I think they cut out any heart the show had, by cutting anything they perceived slowed up the action.

Sometimes, audiences need respite from relentless up-tempo numbers and franticly fast storytelling. There was a wonderful ballad that Pippa Grandison's character Sukie sang to my daughter's character, beautifully played by Penny McNamee. The song was 'Loose Ends' and it was perfectly placed in Act Two, with great depth of storytelling. It was cut a couple of weeks in. In my opinion, that was a mistake. I sometimes include 'Loose Ends' in concerts to this day.

In 2004, I played Desirée in *A Little Night Music* again in New Zealand, for Canterbury Opera, where Brian had been artistic director for a number of years. Canterbury Opera's home was Christchurch, but we played both Christchurch and Auckland, in the premiere production of this show in New Zealand.

Although opera singers spend their careers returning to roles, time after time in some cases, I had never done it. Of course, this was my third outing of this fabulous piece, having played Petra in 1973–74 in the Australian premiere, and then Desirée for the Sydney Theatre Company in 1991, when Toni Collette was a wonderful Petra.

It was fascinating to me that I didn't really have to relearn the dialogue. It was all there. It had been a long time between drinks, but that muscle memory leapt into gear. Just as all those bad things that happen to us years before are merely in hibernation, ready to burst out and upset us if we allow them to, it seems all the roles we've played are still living inside us. All those lines we've thought we've forgotten are still committed to our memory. They are simply asleep. They've never gone entirely. I find that comforting.

Being an opera company, we didn't wear body microphones. We relied on a few microphones along the front of the stage to enhance the sound. There was the Christchurch Symphony Orchestra to sing over, so the key of Desirée's famous Act Two song 'Send In the Clowns' was a full tone higher than in the original score. I did endeavour to give a fresh reading, to be in the moment, as always. This was thirteen years after my last Desirée. I had more life experience and this was an entirely new company and new production. So I needed to respect that and trust the material.

All of the reviews were wonderful. Perhaps I should revisit roles more often.

The thing I love most about the theatre is that you had to be there. That is the thing I dislike most as well; that is, if you weren't there. We have many great actors captured on film and television and they are true records of performances. Live theatre is a different story. But that is what makes it so special. You had to be there.

What makes the evening or afternoon for that matter so unique is that that particular group of people will never sit together again and react together again for all of time. Every performer and every audience create the atmosphere together. Is there some sort of mysterious pact? Why is it that sometimes an audience reacts as one? And yet, sometimes, there are pockets of laughter coming from different areas? Sometimes, the audience decides to be a quiet audience, as one. It has always fascinated me. Of course, one's timing can be slightly off as a performer and that results in a not so big reaction to a moment, but sometimes it is simply a random thing that happens, a secret, silent conversation between a performer and audience that sets the scene for the night. I love it when I have been performing a show eight times a week for a long time and one day, for some reason, I decide to play a line slightly differently and there is a huge laugh that follows. There are always new things to discover about a role, new motivations to discover, new ways of playing a moment, new choices to make. Performing is never boring.

There is nothing that can compete with live performance. It is not always

life changing, or even wonderful. But we certainly recall that day when
it was. That is why we keep returning. We are hoping that today will be
one of those performances we will never forget, one of those life-changing
moments that only the theatre can give us.

We long for one of those rare nights that we speak of for years to come, as
we say to friends, 'You had to be there.'

18

New Sun in the Sky

It is 2003. I am appearing in an experimental piece about refugees and our treatment of them, called These People for the Sydney Theatre Company at The Wharf Theatre. It is a four hander. In one of my favourite scenes, we are dressed as penguins, being turned back at the border for not having our papers in order. It is a black comedy.

At this time, the Sydney Theatre, now called the Roslyn Packer Theatre, has almost finished completion. During our season of this little gem, Robyn Nevin, still artistic director of STC tells me about some groups of benefactors, the Board, some other folk, some notables, who are planning to do a walk through of the new theatre on some sort of open day, finishing with a drink and so on. She tells me they are calling the rehearsal room the Richard Wherrett Rehearsal Room, and Robyn asks me if I will stand in the rehearsal room, with a piano, and sing 'All That Jazz', as visitors move through the rehearsal room throughout the day.

'After all, Chicago remains one of the STC's most successful productions,' she says.

That is true, but I'm not wild about that idea.

𝒆𝒆

Earlier that year, 2003, I appeared in a Melbourne Theatre Company, Sydney Theatre Company production of a sensational Hannie Rayson play called *Inheritance*. I had the best time. Directed by Simon Phillips, it is a brilliant family saga, with themes about the raping of our lands and our disenfranchisement of Indigenous people.

One of the things I will never forget, apart from the cast's weekend coach trip out to the north-west of Victoria during rehearsals so that we could all drink in the atmosphere of the setting of the play, a great memory, was our marching as a cast, against the proposed war in Iraq (for all the good it did).

The company taking part in the protest actually appeared on the rehearsal schedule. We finished rehearsals early that day and taxis were waiting to take us all to the meeting point for the march through the city of Melbourne. How fantastic that was of the MTC! Ever the activist, I was extremely proud to be a part of this company at this moment in time.

I played a countrywoman who was largely uneducated, but entitled and political, a sort of Pauline Hanson in the making, a fabulous role, which I relished. Pauline Hanson is an independent politician in Australia with right-wing views and is considered by some to be a 'nut job', although she has lots of followers. There is a scene in *Inheritance* when my character, Maureen, becomes the politician in front of our eyes as her husband, played wonderfully by Steve Bisley, backs up his ute so she can give a rousing political speech, standing on the tray. The speech is so shocking in its content, but so hysterically funny, that I don't think we ever got through it in the rehearsal room without collapsing into gales of laughter, while Simon Phillips tried to keep it together. Though the tears running down his face as he tried to stifle his laughter were a dead give away. All in all, this was a fine cast of actors at the top of their game. We were a smash in both Melbourne and Sydney.

Towards the end of that year was when Brian and I moved to Moss Vale, in the Southern Highlands of New South Wales, halfway (a little closer to Sydney) between Sydney and Canberra, but commutable to both cities. I had longed for a cool-climate garden to grow roses, peonies, lilacs, rhododendrons, and so on. Also, I was over Sydney. That summer humidity was far too much a reminder of my upbringing in Brisbane, where, in

February, with the hideous humidity, we were made to wear stockings, gloves and hats to school. Dry heat is much better for my asthma.

Although sometimes it can be tiresome commuting, I am always happy to be on that road home from the city. When we lived in the inner city, I used to drive to nurseries at Dural, a semi-rural outer suburb of Sydney, with larger properties and lack of high-rise. There was a point in that journey when I always breathed in and breathed out and felt a sense of freedom. I knew I would be happy, some day, to be in the midst of a beautiful landscape each day. There are many show business folk, a lot of them friends, who have moved to the Highlands now. It is a good life. I am certain my mother would have loved visiting. She loved roses, as do I. I have over a hundred, mostly heritage, all with perfume.

Around the time of moving here, I drove to Canberra to have lunch with Caroline Stacey, who had directed me in *The Vagina Monologues* a few years before, and Brian had used her to direct *Lakme* for Canterbury Opera in Christchurch.

She had been appointed artistic director of The Street Theatre in Canberra, which is reminiscent of Belvoir Theatre in Sydney. I was talking to Caroline about an idea I had for a musical based on my mother and me. I thought nothing more about it until Caroline contacted me about the notion of joining their writer's program, called The Hive, where I would get feedback and regular dramaturgy.

That is just what happened.

I began writing. Over the next few years, right up to 2014, I was a part of that writing group and a regular performer at The Street. In between my other acting and singing commitments, I drove down to Canberra on a regular basis to take part in workshops, developments, and to direct some developing works. Also, I appeared in some major works for Caroline over the next few years.

Jacques Brel is Alive and Well and Living in Paris is a show I had always wanted to do. I have since directed a production of my own. Like Kurt Weill's material, I had always adored the songs of Brel. When Caroline Stacey asked me to be in it, I was thrilled. We were critically acclaimed and it was an altogether fantastic experience. It included being invited to the Belgian

Embassy for lunch. Caroline had invited the ambassador and entourage to the opening. They had accepted with trepidation.

'Australians doing Brel? Surely that cannot work!' they said to us at lunch that day.

However, they were all pleasantly surprised at our expertise and commitment to the authenticity of this material. Hence the invitation to lunch! They served the best chocolate I have ever tasted that day at the Belgian Embassy.

I was the actor in the huge experiment that is *White Rabbit, Red Rabbit* for the Street, something I found an exhilarating and unique experience, as well as playing the lead in Alana Valentine's wonderful play, *MP* and Tom Davis's play, *The Chain Bridge*, which was born out of our writing group.

My musical play about my mother and me, *Drama Queen*, which had had a rocky start as I changed collaborators and the feel of the piece, ended up enjoying three workshops and a presentation with an audience. The presentation happened with the first writing team, but now, with my new composer, Greg Crease, I believe we have the best version. Mother's songs are all written in the vaudeville style, while Daughter's songs are pure musical theatre. The entire show is written as a vaudeville routine.

My other play, with music, with my collaborator, Greg Crease, is called *Woman's Best Friend*. We had a reading with some wonderful performers, including my long-term friend, Nancye Hayes and me in the central roles. We had a Q and A with the audience afterwards in Sydney in 2016. This is a show we have written for five women, mostly over fifty years of age. I believe it has legs commercially speaking. It concerns women's friendships, a dog park, tree changers, lies, betrayal but, above all, our unconditional love for our pets, something close to my heart.

I intend to keep writing whatever else happens in my life. Writing saves me. My adored dogs save me as well. I love solving problems and that is largely what writing is about. It is certainly what directing is about. That is why I am at my happiest in the safety of a rehearsal room, with the freedom to explore, as opposed to the slog and regimentation of an eight-show week. Mind you, the family atmosphere that a long run of a musical provides is comforting to someone like me who loves to belong, has always wanted to belong.

I wish I had started directing years ago, but my busy performing career didn't leave much time for that. Apart from mentoring and directing shows for Miranda Musical Society, I have, so far, directed and devised some cabaret shows for some performers, some concerts, and have directed two Mozart operas for the Yarra Valley Opera Festival.

In August 2005, I was asked to play the title role in a new Australian musical called *Rosie*. The composer was Peter Stannard, who had been one of the collaborators of the 1958 classic Australian musical, *Lola Montez*.

This show was about the life of a Sydney identity, Rosie Shaw, who was a flower seller in Sydney's Martin Place and had serenaded passers-by and her customers for over forty years with operatic arias and popular tunes. This was an independent production, with the luxury of having Peter Stannard at rehearsals with us most days. I think it was a mistake to use the book writer as the director. It needed an independent eye and it needed a dramaturg. The show was brimming with wonderful melodies and we had assembled a fine cast. We played the Independent Theatre in North Sydney. The fact that it was such a good role, and that the great Stannard had written the piece, was enough reason to agree to it.

We didn't do well. I fear, as often happens with these sorts of productions, the producers had raised enough money for pre-production, for theatre costs, for payment of the performers, musicians, sound and lighting, but did not have enough in the budget to sell the show, for publicity, for press or television advertisements, for all the things that are required to get bums on seats.

We did have much fun, especially with some of the choreography. I admired Peter Stannard so much. He has left us now, unfortunately. My friend and colleague, Alan Burke, who had been a collaborator on *Lola Montez* with Stannard, and had directed me all those years before in that televised version of *The Sentimental Bloke*, saw the show, but died not long after.

Meanwhile, my life in the Southern Highlands was about to take a turn. I was asked by a group of people to run for council.

I had been outspoken about the council wanting to sell off green space and had written to the local newspaper and had several letters published. I am not anti-development, but anti what I consider inappropriate development. I am happy for hordes to move here to this beautiful place and have no doubt that, with the expansion of Sydney and the unaffordability of the inner city in Sydney, more families will be attracted to our part of the world, south-west of the city. However, we need more infrastructure, more schools, certainly more frequent and faster trains to the city, as there is not enough work locally for many people, except hedging people – they charge like wounded bulls!

I was running for council on a ticket that wanted to keep 'the green between' the villages and towns, so that the beauty of the Highlands is maintained, with infill housing in the towns and villages, rather than becoming a huge, sprawling outer suburb of Sydney and losing green space. Also, I had been working for a number of years on a multi-arts festival for our area, with me as the first artistic director. I had spoken to Hugh Jackman about coming on board in some capacity. There are many high-profile theatricals living in the area now, so I hoped to be able to use their expertise and get them interested in the festival. We had a Board and regular meetings. We had a multitude of ideas; in fact, we had decided on a wonderful program for the first festival. We had many people interested. But finding and locking in money for such a festival was almost impossible. I thought if I were an elected official, perhaps I could be in a position to put pressure on council and the state government for some grants for such a festival.

I didn't win. I almost won. There are nine councillors in Wingecarribee Shire. I came in seventh past the post. However, I did not have my preferences sorted. So with preferences counted, I fell to tenth place, just short of a place on council.

During my campaign, I spoke to Neville Wran and asked him if he could help by speaking to the Labor Party branch in the shire to set up a preference deal. He obliged, but contacted me a few weeks later, saying that, embarrassingly, someone in my team had leaked that we had already done a deal with Labor. The upshot was that I had inadvertently embarrassed Mr Wran, something I hated doing, and the preference deal had fallen through as a result of interference. I had no choice but to take the high ground and to not do any preference deals with anyone.

I do remember very well waking up the day after that election and looking at the photographs of the newly elected councillors on the front page of the local rag, feeling a huge sense of relief, knowing instinctively that I had dodged a bullet. I would have served to the best of my ability for the four-year term, but I knew I would have been voted down constantly on things that I considered important. 'Arts. What's that?'

This council understands the visual arts very well. There is a powerful visual arts lobby, made up of many famous voices, famous painters who live in the area, fighting for galleries to be built, and there is an arts trail that happens each spring. But the performing arts keeps getting put on the backburner, although many residents in the area are avid theatre goers and would support a new theatre if we could find the funds.

I had been surprised at how well I had spoken at rallies and public meetings. Actors are used to interpreting the words of others and creating believable characters, not necessarily making inspiring speeches. I knew I was good at talking to audiences in an off-the-cuff manner in a cabaret setting so perhaps this helped. Also, I was authentic in my delivery and honest in my answering of questions. I never dodged a question the way politicians are in the habit of doing. I was a straight talker, no BS. People knew, even if they disagreed with certain of my policies, I was the real deal.

I count this period as one of my happiest. I had stepped out of my comfort zone and the best part of it was that I was connecting and getting to know my community, rather than being someone from the big city who had moved to the country, but had not engaged with locals. I made many friends during this campaign. I felt I had earned the right to say that my home was the Southern Highlands.

I worked for some years on the festival idea to no avail. Now I have moved on to lobbying for a multi-arts centre to be built, so that the Highlands can take its place on the national theatre touring circuit. That would be a good start. It is some years off, I fear. However, I will not give up.

19

One Life to Live

It is 2009. I am in Griffith in New South Wales when I receive the news from my brother, Leigh that our brother Ray has died suddenly of a heart attack at his home in Brisbane.

I am on tour with a stellar cast. We are doing a capital cities and regional tour of Robert Harling's play **Steel Magnolias**. I am playing Ouisa.

Ever the actress, the first person I call is my stage manager. I know we have no understudies. We have already had problems when one member of the cast ends up in hospital during the Sydney season and another actress goes on with a book. She is on for a few nights, learns the show on the run and is brilliant. I know how difficult it is to replace me if I decide to go to the funeral and take some time out, as the company is now touring in the regions, so it is not so simple to get another actress here, rehearse her in and get her on the stage. The thought of it is so stressful, the thought of letting the cast down that is, that I decide to stay with the company, not attend the funeral, and to sit in a quiet place in a park on the day. By then, we are in Wagga.

Mum, Dad, Noel, Ralph, and now Ray ... all gone suddenly from heart attacks. Leigh and I are the only remaining from our immediate family. Think I'll get my heart checked. I do when I finish this tour. My heart is fine.

It had been many years since I had been on a regional tour. Not since I began my career with Queensland Theatre Company and toured that state, had I even considered such a tour. But this was a wonderful part and a great group of women of profile to play with. I had recorded my second Sondheim album, *The Stephen Sondheim Songbook, Volume 2*, but it had been a while since I had done a straight play. We played Sydney, Melbourne, Launceston, Brisbane and Adelaide as well as some major regional cities in all states.

It is a privilege to bring good theatre to the regions. Communities are so appreciative. There are some wonderful arts centres throughout Australia that need to be filled with product of a professional standard. During this tour and much later, during the tour of my one-woman show, *Turner's Turn*, I have noticed vast gaps in the standards of the various arts centres and theatres and the way they are run.

Usually, local councils are in charge of these theatres, with managers employed by the councils. I have found that the best results – that is, sold out seasons, excitement in the community about the show – happen when the managers of these arts centres have some sort of theatrical background, or at least a love of theatre, and are not simply council employees.

When you arrive in a town, do a walk around, and notice posters in shop windows and a buzz around town about the upcoming performances, you know that you are going to fill the theatre and the locals are in for a great night. On the other hand, when you arrive in a town and find it difficult to find a poster anywhere, you realise that locals know nothing about the show, and your heart sinks. You become aware that the management of the arts centre, whose salary is paid whether your show does well or not, does not give a fig! It is disappointing.

However, when it works, it really works. It seems everyone in the town turns up for a great night out. That is exactly what happened when we were in Griffith for *Steel Magnolias*. This audience, and people had driven in from Hay and other environs, was one of the best audiences I have ever witnessed. We landed every laugh and they went wild at our curtain call and threw us a wonderful party afterwards.

The next day, I received the news about my brother. We moved on to Wagga for the next show and I spent some quiet time, thinking of Ray and of all the family I had lost. It was comforting, at least, to know that my parents had died before their children. I don't think my mother could have coped with losing her children. She was an incredibly difficult, infuriating woman. She didn't know how to show us love, or to ever say that she loved us, or even know how to touch us physically in any kind of loving way. But I have no doubt that she cared. How? I have no idea. I just know.

I recall playing Coffs Harbour on this tour, in a dinky little gem of a theatre. We ended up having a brilliant, short season, even though the town had been cut in half by floods when we were there. Also, someone had sent the wrong measurements of the theatre. Our set, even though we toured with two versions, one larger, one smaller, did not fit the stage at all.

We placed the set on the floor of the auditorium and proceeded to do the show in very close proximity to our audience, having to lose only a few rows of seats in the process. Touring like this presents its challenges. You have to be adaptable.

The long tour of *Steel Magnolias* finished in Adelaide at Her Majesty's Theatre in Grote Street. The theatre has since been restored to its former glory. I have happy memories of performing there with several shows over the years: of getting to the theatre really early during a famous Adelaide heatwave, just to feel the air conditioning; about a cast member of a show in Adelaide visiting a clairvoyant who told her she was going to have an accident. She immediately cancelled her planned weekend of horse riding. Then, after a matinee at the theatre, we were on our way to dinner, she stepped off the kerb, twisted her ankle and broke it.

We had got on well during that *Steel Magnolias* tour, all those opinionated women. No fallings out; well, not for long. You have to get on when you are travelling so closely together, mostly picking up rental cars at airports and driving together for long distances to towns, finding where the hotels are, living on your wits, while missing family back home. I am thankful that I have seen many parts of Australia I would never have seen without such tours.

We didn't play Western Australian towns on this tour, but some years later, with *Turner's Turn*, which I continue to tour with my musical director for that show, Brad Miller, I have played from Kalgoorlie to Esperance, as well as seasons in several venues in Perth. We continue to play this show six years after opening it in Sydney. It is the kind of show you can keep in a trunk and bring out when necessary.

When we were in Kalgoorlie, an historic town I am thankful to have visited, as I never thought I would, we were told on arrival at the beautiful arts centre that our audience was very small, hardly any bookings. I asked why. The woman who ran this gorgeous theatre, said, 'Nothing does well here. Sometimes a stand-up comedian does well.'

What struck me was the casual statement, the acceptance, the lack of any care about the situation, let alone a willingness to try to bring in audiences, or to try to change the status quo. Perhaps she had tried in the past but was at the 'giving up' stage. But her living did not depend on getting a full house. We had been there for two days. I could have done some radio or press. Perhaps it would not have made a difference. At least, it may have helped. Or perhaps she should never have booked my show.

There needs to be a panel of people with arts backgrounds employed to tour the country, advising arts centres about what sorts of shows are appropriate for certain towns and about ways to build audiences. There is no point in constructing all these wonderful arts centres simply to tick an 'Arts' box and then do nothing but buy in the five or so shows on offer that year, whether those shows are right for that community or not.

There is something intrinsically wrong with the way the system works at the moment. These beautiful theatres exist all over the country and need product, but we should have people who are at least interested in the theatre in charge, or people who have enjoyed professional theatre careers, either as performers, or backstage. Council employees, more often than not, do not cut the mustard!

By the way, the manager of the Kalgoorlie Theatre did not watch my show, which our small audience loved. We received a standing ovation that night. But that manager missed out on it all. She remained in her office while my show was on, catching up on paperwork.

Some of the newly built theatres all around the country do not seem to have ever received advice, or perhaps they've ignored advice, from theatre experts. When I played the fairly new theatre in Springwood, in the Blue Mountains of New South Wales, the loading dock was down three flights of stairs, with no lift! It didn't matter for our show, but any play or ballet or opera or musical theatre performance would have a set to be lugged up three flights of stairs by hand – madness!

Also, there was no hoarding, no place on the outside of the theatre to place a sign or poster. The building looks like a library or an office building. And there is little to no wing space.

I remember being amused by our sound technician's take on my comments about a Russian ballet company they had enjoyed there recently. I said, 'How did a ballet company cope with no wing space?' I know that dancers need space enough to leap off stage without running into a wall.

'They are professionals,' he quipped in a knowing manner.

I considered myself told!

The best thing, the privilege of regional touring, is the knowledge that you have given your talents to people who are starved of a lot of live performance. All audiences recognise quality, no matter where they are from.

I trust that these tours continue, that the standards of performance are upheld, that the managements of the arts centres throughout this vast country are educated about what artists require, and what is required from them in choosing and selling shows, and that theatre fan numbers from regional towns and cities continue to grow.

I have toured many cabaret shows, within Australia and around the world. My concert and cabaret career have been very important to me throughout my life. During the down times with theatre, television and film work, I have always been able to be proactive, creating new shows I can pull out of the trunk, as it were, and perform. My cabaret shows began with *Geraldine Turner Sings*, that notion of Bill Shanahan's that had transferred to New York.

I have appeared in cabaret in several countries: the US, Africa, Canada, the UK and in Germany, in an original, Victorian spiegeltent in Berlin.

I loved playing Berlin, performing in the home of cabaret. Brian accompanied me for that tour. Our first night in town, we went to the venue to catch another act and get a feel for the venue. When my first night in this fabulous city included a German singing group singing 'Falling in Love Again', the famous Marlene Dietrich song, I thought I'd died and gone to heaven.

Our dressing room was an old gypsy caravan from the late 1800s. We stayed in a neighbourhood in the former East Berlin. We felt as if we were immersed in the city. It is a fascinating place, riddled with history and reminders of World War Two at every turn, as you round a corner and a building is missing, bombed and never replaced. Also, we couldn't help but notice that people talked of the war every day. One night after the show we were chatting and I asked our employers why this was so. They simply said, 'Of course. We must never forget what we did.'

After our final night, we sat down with the accountant from the venue, who paid us in cash, a first for me. I believe this occurs on a regular basis in Germany.

We flew to Vienna for a break (to have schnitzel and sachertorte) and to meet up with some friends, and on to New York to see some shows.

Steve Sondheim called to have a chat with me while we were in New York, a wonderful surprise. The disagreements about the second Sondheim album had been relegated to the past, thankfully. Steve was always generous of heart.

He apologised for not being able to have us over as he was having some minor surgery that week. I must have gasped at that news. He assured me it was simply a removal of a couple of skin lesions from his face.

We chatted for a long time on the phone. It was lovely to have a casual conversation with him. We talked about ideas, and the fact that almost everything is stolen from somewhere else and how that is a fine thing. The notion of an original idea is an impossible one to reconcile. We discussed this at length and agreed that you can come up with an idea and develop it into something that ends up being perceived as yours.

We talked about all things theatre and about the first time we had met, during that International Theatre Forum in Sydney many years before. Steve remembered everything, the date, the address of the house we had supper in, all the names of the people who were there and what was talked about that night. His memory was much more detailed than mine.

I raved about playing Berlin to him, actually raved about how much I loved Berlin. He had been there only once, but found it unappealing. I can understand that. I think it is a city you have to stay in for a few weeks to get a real feel for it. Steve had been there for a few days only. We were lucky enough to meet some wonderful people from Bar jeder Vernunft, the Berlin venue where we had played our cabaret show for three weeks, so we had been told the places we should seek out and where the interesting, unusual shopping districts were and which galleries not to miss, which parts of the city to visit. We had the time to drink in the city. As I raved on about my love of Berlin and of playing there, Steve accepted my review of the city with grace.

Fast-forward to 26 November 2021 and I was reeling from the news that many had dreaded. We had lost a giant in losing Stephen Sondheim. Musical theatre will never be the same without that cutting-edge trailblazer, that extraordinary composer and brilliant observer of the human condition. I remain so grateful to have known him, to have met him when I was a young performer, to possess so much correspondence over the years, to have met with him on several happy occasions, to have continued to enjoy a relationship with him over many decades and to have played many of the sensational roles he wrote for women.

I am left with the memory of a kind man, who was a true mentor, generous to a fault; a man who wished the best for anyone pursuing a life in the theatre, a man who adored and respected talent, a creator in every sense of the word, a man of fierce intelligence – as I said, a giant of the theatre. We will certainly never see the like again. I will continue to miss him.

During that same visit to New York after our Berlin season, we met up with composer Ervin Drake and his lovely wife, Edith. Brian had contacted Ervin about the possibility of me recording one of his songs, 'The Wrong Man', from his musical, *Her First Roman*, and about Brian's ideas for a totally different feel of the song. I was thankful we weren't having that conversation about changing musical arrangements with Steve Sondheim.

We did record the song but it was never released. Ervin, of course, had written songs like 'I Believe' and 'It Was a Very Good Year'. He had much to say about Sinatra. He had spent a lot of time with him and held him in high esteem.

Ervin took us to The Friar's Club for dinner. That was special in itself. The most interesting thing for me about the whole experience was hearing about Edith's and his history. Edith had been his first love, when they were both very young. She had ended the relationship suddenly and it had broken his heart. So he sat down and wrote the lyrics for 'Good Morning Heartache', which Billie Holiday went on to record and make famous. It is one of my favourite songs, with the most heart-rending lyric.

Ervin eventually married someone else and had a family, as did Edith. Both their spouses had died not long before we met them. Ervin had written a note to Edith saying how sorry he was to hear about her husband's passing. She wrote back. They met up again and married soon after. Edith told us that night that being married to Ervin was like being on a date all the time. How divine!

So we were having dinner with the person who had written that iconic song, 'Good Morning Heartache', and with the person the song had been written about! I had to pinch myself.

I was a little weary after that trip and that cabaret season in Berlin. However, I had surprised myself that I had seemed just as at ease with a German audience as I had with an audience whose first language is English. I enjoy the intimacy of cabaret and relish the opportunity to be myself on stage. Cabaret remains a majorly successful part of my work.

I have had the great fortune to be supported by the critics over the years for my cabaret, concert and theatre work, but I have had some shockers, some truly bad reviews. I haven't kept any of them but I do remember the ones that were personal attacks. I received a review for a cabaret show once, part of which read, 'She pretends to be a lovely person up there, but we know what she is really like.'

Needless to say, that particular critic had never met me.

I always have trouble going on stage the night after a bad review has been published. Any missed laugh, any slight mistiming or lack of reaction makes me imagine, rightly or wrongly, that the audience has read that review and believes everything in it.

By the next night, I have usually tossed it off as tomorrow's fish and chips, as my mother used to say. She also used to say never to get upset about people copying you. 'While people are copying you, they'll never get ahead of you.'

True, Mother. I hear you.

These days, with social media, everyone is a critic. No longer do we have folk with some sort of expertise and knowledge of the theatre writing reviews, or even writing real sentences. We must endure entitled idiots publishing uninformed garbage online about us. It is best to never read them. I do wish I had a thicker skin. I've been performing for well over fifty years and yet, all those feelings of inadequacy, which I am sure stem from my mother, still lurk just under the surface.

20

No Time at All

I receive a call from my agent in 2011 about taking over as Madam Morrible in Wicked for a few weeks. I have no interest in the role when auditions happen originally. But, since this is a short stint, and dates fit in with my schedule, I agree to do it. It seems Maggie Kirkpatrick (Morrible) is recovering from surgery. She had been in Anything Goes with me and we go way back. I'm happy to step in and help out.

The thing is, they want me on stage in the role, in Brisbane, within three days.

'I can do that,' I say, without really thinking. If I did, I'd throw up.

So, a 'music call', a plane trip while learning lines, costume fittings, a few rehearsals with Karen Johnson Mortimer (she had been in No, No, Nanette all those years before and was now resident director of Wicked) and I am on stage in a matinee performance the following Sunday, with an assistant stage manager in tow, saying, 'Now! Go!' as each cue happens and my stomach hits the floor.

This show is a well-oiled machine by the time I go in. I rehearse. I get to do a dress rehearsal, for me, with the tricks and lighting and all of the principals, including some ensemble players who speak lines in my scenes.

It is surreal enough being flung on so quickly, but to my astonishment, during that first performance in my first scene, there are people I've never seen before on stage, some walking past me as I speak. So disconcerting. Who are those extra

people? I just have to focus and get through it. I manage. I am like a train heading
for the final station as I whip through the scenes and costume and wig changes,
while endeavouring to play the character and be in the moment.

Bert Newton (sadly gone now) is playing The Wizard. He makes a wonderful
curtain speech welcoming me to the company and sharing with the audience that,
from start to finish, it has been three days. A huge ovation follows. I end up doing
most of the Brisbane season, and it is decided I do half of the Adelaide season, sharing
each performance week with Maggie in Adelaide, as she recovers.

It was great to be back in Brisbane with *Wicked*. Some of my extended family
came to see the show, which I grew to love, especially the positive messages
in it for young girls. It was a terrific company. It turned out to be a great role
for me and I wondered why I had never considered it. Partly, it was because
it was not really a singing role. That had been my prerequisite for accepting
a role in a musical – at least one solo for me.

Playing this character role and finding moments within that to make the
role mine, such as singing more of the role than is usually done, still meant
that I didn't have to be overly concerned about my voice, which was the
usual, disciplined way of life during a musical in an eight-show week when
you have lots of songs to do. In fact, during this season and in Adelaide,
more often than not, we played a nine-show week. Such was the success of
the show. So, although it was a busy time, it was a very happy time because
I had the luxury of being able to have a social life, not having to worry
about getting a cold or my voice getting tired. When you are starring in a
big musical and carrying the show, your life is a solitary one, as you must
remain show fit by virtually putting your life on hold for the sake of the
show.

I was offered the role again for the tour to Asia, but decided at the time, it
was too long to be away from Brian and the dogs. At least within Australia,
you can get back for a weekend every few weeks, not at all possible if you
are in a different country.

The final season of that production was in Perth. I was put on standby for that. The court case, which poor Maggie had to endure, was about to break as a news story. It concerned a fan alleging some sort of sexual abuse. I guess the management was building in an extra protection in case the worst happened. I contacted Maggie and gave her my total support as soon as I heard about the ridiculous charges. I had known her for many years. Her complete innocence was later proven.

I spent the next couple of years working at The Street Theatre in Canberra, appearing in various plays and directing some workshops of new Australian works, which was extremely satisfying. Time flew.

Then, in 2014, Meredith O'Reilly contacted me out of the blue. She, along with Katrina Retallick, Lisa Freshwater (director) and Alistair Thomson were producing an independent musical, *Ruthless!*, at the Seymour Centre in Sydney. I knew the piece; some years before, it had been sent to me as a possible vehicle, when I was young enough to play the central role. A production hadn't come to fruition at that time. The show, while having a central role, is really an ensemble piece.

All the roles in this show are worthy and funny and fabulous. It also includes a role for a talented young girl. It is high camp in its nature, with a terrific score. I hesitated at first, as they wanted me to play what most would describe as a cameo role, the role of theatre critic, Lita Encore. It was Brian who convinced me to play the role, which he considered to be the best part in the show. There is no responsibility of carrying the show. Nevertheless, it is a star turn, if someone with my ability and history has the opportunity to bring a career on stage with her. A musical theatre star should play this role. There are many gags to land, but really, the specialty number 'I Hate Musicals' is so much more hilarious, if played by someone who obviously loves musicals and has a vast repertoire of career hits to draw upon.

We had the best time. The season did well. We heard many belly laughs from the audiences every night. Always a plus. The cast was fabulous, particularly Margi De Ferranti. She was hysterical as the schoolteacher. I won a theatre award for playing Lita Encore, as did Katrina Retallick for playing the central role. She was wonderful in it.

A tour was spoken of, and I believe we would have done well in Melbourne and Brisbane at the very least. However, Katrina was pregnant and, sensibly, they didn't wish to recast. By the time she'd had the baby, and by the time it could be attempted to raise the money, arrange the schedules, theatres booked, the impetus had gone. I have always believed it was a missed opportunity. Timing is everything.

Later that year, I appeared in a gala concert of *Side by Side by Sondheim*, with a large cast at the Theatre Royal in Sydney for producer, Enda Markey. It was the first time I had met him. Following this, he asked me to do a small tour of this marvellous show. We played Sydney, Canberra and Geelong, at the Geelong Performing Arts Centre, GPAC.

How many times had I been to Melbourne? I had lived and worked there for years on end. Yet I had never been to Geelong. It had developed into quite a hub of the arts over the years. I had no idea it was even on the water, on the bay. We played the smaller theatre, while the Belvoir production of *Death of a Salesman*, played the larger theatre.

Many of us from the two casts stayed at the same hotel and many a night the divine Colin Friels, who was playing the lead in the Arthur Miller play 'held court' in the bar at the hotel until the wee hours. Many tales and much laughter were enjoyed by all of us. I love the way great actors can deliver a tale, always timing the gag at the end perfectly. Our show turned out to be a fabulous tour. That Sondheim material isn't too shabby either.

The wonderful Michael Falzon, who was to die tragically a few years later of a rare cancer, was part of our cast. Gone far too soon; life is short.

This was the beginning of my friendship with Enda Markey. He continued to produce my show, *Turner's Turn*. He has done so for the last few years. It is a show I can rehearse at a moment's notice, with my musical director, Brad Miller.

In 2019, Brad and I were performing the one act, ninety-minute version of the show at a Morning Melodies at The Clocktower in Moonie Ponds in Melbourne. It was a full house. The show was going very well. I was in good voice and was particularly funny that day. My confidence was up. It was one of those performances when you seem to land every gag. The audience reaction was great.

More than three-quarters of the way through the show, actually with about five songs to go, I had completed a ballad in a pin spot. Blackout. Applause. I took one step forward in the blackout to introduce the next song.

Obviously, I had not realised how far downstage I was. The stage manager said later that she was praying I would not take a step forward. Mind you, there was no luminous tape marking along the front of the stage, which usually is there to enable a performer to see in a blackout. As I took a step, my life went into slow motion while the support underneath me gave way to nothingness.

I fell off the stage.

The arm of a chair in the front row broke my fall. It could have been much worse. My left side, in fact my ribs, took the brunt of it. Thank goodness there was no-one sitting in that particular chair. I remember saying, quite loudly, 'I'm really hurt.'

Houselights came up. The audience was led out. An ambulance was called. Audience members passed by and patted me, wishing me well as I lay on the floor, unable to move, with the pain really kicking in. I later found out that not one person asked for their money back.

That day was a series of firsts. 1. I had never fallen off a stage in a more than fifty-year career. 2. I had never been in an ambulance. 3. I had never worked for a producer who supported me in a way that went beyond what an employer would normally do, apart from Cameron carrying my luggage to the limo, when I became ill during *The Witches of Eastwick*.

Enda was in Sydney. Brad Miller called him within minutes of my accident. He jumped on a plane straight away, flew to Melbourne and sat with me at the hospital. I ended up being there all night, as they needed to do several tests to make sure there were no other injuries, apart from two broken ribs. Enda said that he could book a plane for the following day to get me home. I didn't think I could manage getting in and out of the tight seats in a plane, with all the pain. So Enda hired a large, four-wheel drive so there would be enough room for me to get in and out with limited pain. He drove me home from Melbourne the next day. What a wonderful friend and a caring producer.

I was directing *Les Misérables* for Miranda Musical Society in Sydney at the same time. I had flown to Melbourne to do that concert in between rehearsals. We were about to start the final week's rehearsals, then go into production week. I missed only one rehearsal, and I got through till opening night on painkillers. Broken ribs really hurt. I don't recommend it.

In 2017, I had made my debut with Opera Australia in a pastiche operetta called *Two Weddings, One Bride* that had been adapted by Robert Greene from an opéra bouffe, *Girofle-Girofla* by Charles Lecocq. We had done a workshop the year before. Robert had written the role of the Mother (whose character drives the piece) for me, and my husband was to be played by the wonderful character actor, Robert Alexander, whom I had not worked with since the early days of Sydney Theatre Company.

The notion was to have two older actors at the centre of the show, surrounded by fabulous young opera singers, particularly the dual leading roles of our twin daughters, beautifully played by either Julie Lea Goodwin or Zoe Drummond.

The workshop went well and I was heartened by the fact that my songs could be played in a musical theatre way, though, of course, there were many ensembles to sing. This was not a problem for me at all, blending with other voices. I have done so for my entire life.

Unfortunately, by the time we started rehearsals, darling Robert had become ill and had to withdraw. In fact, he died and I must say his funeral was the best, most joyous funeral I have ever attended, full of hilarious stories, readings, and loving tributes. Only performers can produce a great send-off like that. It was a true celebration of a life. People flew in from all over the country. There was standing room and the room was filled with so many sensational performers, writers, and directors, all there for Robert. That room was brimming with love.

I hoped and made my feelings clear to Robert Greene, that the company would hire an actor to play my husband, to keep the balance that he had intended, and to not leave me to be the only actor amongst a cast of opera singers. Memories of opera voices mixed with musical theatre voices and the bad reviews for *La Belle Hélène* flooded back.

They didn't cast an actor. They cast an opera singer, John Bolton Wood, whom I had not worked with since the first production of *A Little Night*

Music back in 1973–74. So, to me, the balance was not what had originally been intended; that is two actors as the parents, surrounded by young opera singers.

Robert Greene, who had written the piece, had changed his name a couple of years earlier. Formerly, he had been known as Andrew Greene and was to have been the musical director of that first cancelled season of *Gypsy*, so it was really nice to come full circle and work with him after all this time.

Three separate seasons at the Playhouse at Sydney Opera House settled in well, and we ended up having a lovely time playing this fast moving, ensemble show, brimming with marvellous operetta songs and melodies, and farcical, madcap comedy.

In 2019, we played the show again in Melbourne at the Playhouse at the Arts Centre, followed by a short season at Riverside Theatre at Parramatta in Sydney. Brian was in charge, musically, for that season and played piano for that short tour. It was lovely to have him on board.

In no time at all, you move from being the youngest in the cast, to someone young cast members look up to. It happens in a flash. You find yourself talking about something in a coffee break and you notice that young cast members are hanging on every word. It is a bizarre thing and it is extraordinary to realise just how far you have travelled in a long career and how you must keep on moving forward and reinventing yourself if you want to keep working.

An ingenue for instance, who doesn't move into another way to be, can have a five-year career, then disappear, as there is already another young girl climbing the ranks to replace her. It is vital to stay ahead of the game, not to play catch-up.

If you're lucky enough to enjoy longevity in a career, nothing can replace the absolute satisfaction of a great performance and the love, yes, love, of a truly appreciative audience.

21

Looking for the Light

We're back in 1992. I am devastated by the first production of Gypsy being cancelled. Little do I know at this point, that six productions of Gypsy are to go up in smoke. I seek help from a psychologist. I see her over the next couple of years, while missing a lot of sessions because of work commitments and tours.

We talk a great deal about my mother, my early life and my feelings of abandonment throughout my life. In fact, I realise I have always been afraid, of almost everything. I believe I suffer from a form of PTSD from my mother's treatment of me when I was young. Being locked in a cupboard as punishment is not good for starters. However, I am very skilled at pretending all is well. I am an actress after all. I have used that poker face my whole life. It serves me well when people are hurtful. I am the queen of the poker face. I have been since I was little, on the bus with my mother.

I come to the conclusion in 1992, that my relationships with men have never really been satisfactory. A year later I meet my husband and things change.

⸎

People have been encouraging me for years to write a few things down as a record. I have been resisting. Writing about your life is your one chance to tell it like it is … like it was.

I have always lived on and off stage in an authentic way. I certainly don't ever wish to write anything 'dry'. Surely, it is not just your career, which, after all, is mostly easily researched, but also your life that is interesting to others: how you see the world, how you see the changes in show business throughout the years you have been working, how you have managed to navigate some sort of a life.

It is the balance that is interesting to me. A life and a career and how you separate the two. Do you? Can you? How much of who I am is my talent, my career? How much of who I am was created by an almost impossible relationship with a desperately unhappy mother and a family that did not encourage me?

Why, when my back is against the wall, a position that can destroy many people, do I find that I am at my best; that I am exhilarated and come out with renewed vigour?

Will I always be a performer till my last breath? Could I find contentment in a garden, with my dogs, with my husband, and a nice house, without having something to create on the boil, or at least on a simmer?

I think not. Creation, art, and the feeling I will always have something to contribute in some way are at the centre of my life and will continue to be, one job at a time. Even in my dotage, I hope that I will be able to contribute in some way, by passing on knowledge, by writing, by mentoring, by simply turning up and lending my voice to important issues.

Thinking back on a long career, I do believe that I have lived and worked through some of the most exciting decades in Australia for the performing arts. I know others of my generation have written of this. I join them in celebrating those years in Australia, when the arts were something to be nurtured and celebrated.

The resurgence of the Australian film industry in the 1970s was due to Gough Whitlam and his extraordinary few years as prime minister. Apart from a multitude of reforms that we still enjoy today, like universal health care for one, his government maintained an absolute belief in the arts and the notion of the arts being capable of nourishing the souls of everyone.

Artistic endeavour used to be held in high esteem by all governments in the last quarter of the twentieth century, and it was something to be cherished. The

ABC had real funding for in-house productions. Theatre companies, big, small, medium, received funds – never enough, but enough to exist and continue to flourish and experiment. Medium-sized arts companies used to tour shows and produce shows on a regular basis. They have all but disappeared, replaced by independent companies, often code for 'we don't pay performers'.

Australian political parties used to have arts launches during election campaigns. Now they don't. Do political parties believe there are no votes in the arts? When did that notion evolve?

During the pandemic in 2020, 2021 and into 2022, the arts were what people all over the world turned to while in lockdown, whether it was reading a book, listening to music, watching a series on television, visiting an art gallery online or a livestream of a performance. We must hold on to that and lobby and work to convince governments that the arts are vital to us all and deserve ongoing funding and support.

In the 1970s, for instance, when Nimrod Theatre in Sydney was about the most exciting place to be, with a new Australian play to see every couple of months and writers like David Williamson emerging, I was in my twenties, a young starlet. Theatre opportunities allowed careers to flourish. Actors/performers did not need to go away and then come home to Australia in order to be respected. The so-called 'cultural cringe' was disappearing as new writers, filmmakers, designers, composers, and performers were suddenly able to stay in Australia and build careers.

These days, at least, the world has opened up more and it is easier to work and live on several continents if you wish. However, I am happy that my career has been forged, in the main, in my own country and that I have been able to continue to make a career in my own country. I am proud of that.

I recall when I was a young girl, a teenager, starting out in Queensland, doing an interview about 'going south and becoming fully professional' and talking about my ambitions for my future. I said my ambition was for Australians to think of me as 'Our Geraldine' in the way that people spoke of the great Gladys Moncrieff as 'Our Glad'.

It makes me smile that the young me even thought to say that, let alone say it out loud to a journalist. Of course, I have not achieved that sort of status by any stretch of the imagination. But I have been searching my mind about what has remained important to me during my career.

It is 'the work'. There is nothing else.

This makes me remember having a coffee and a casual conversation with Hal Prince in New York many years ago, where he spoke about the importance of 'the work'. We agreed that there is good and bad everywhere. People, especially critics, do not always recognise 'great' from 'good' or 'mediocre' from 'really bad'. That is unfortunate. Most things are lumped in together as simply 'an enjoyable night out', or the like. Critics should use more superlatives or real negatives when such words are deserved.

In any case, Hal went on to say that it doesn't matter where you work, on Broadway, in London, in Australia or Europe or Asia, in a large city or a small town, it is 'the work' that is everything.

Hal also said, 'All your life you are trying to get there. Then when you get there, you realise there's no "there" there.'

I heartily agree about 'the work'. It is not how big or how small the company is or where it is. Sometimes we lose sight of that in a world of 'influencers' and 'reality television', endless mediocrity, and people being famous for being famous.

I have been thinking about those moments in the theatre when I have been transported, those moments I have spoken of already, that bring us back and back to the theatre to recapture that feeling. I know there are many more to discover and I am determined to find them.

I like to think that my mother would have been proud that I have managed to continue my career for so long, although I know she never would have said it out loud. I do have her to thank for my work ethic, my commitment, my resilience, my never giving up, even my bolshiness – something these days, I wear as a badge of honour.

You do reach a stage in your life when you must accept you are a grown up. You must stop blaming things that happen on your upbringing. You must step up and take responsibility for your failings. Yet you cannot rip out your past. It is there at every turn, colouring all decisions, holding you back at times. A tiny chink appears and grows and tells you that you're not good enough. At times you are able to erase the chink and you feel confidence flow into your being. It doesn't last. There is a constant fight within you to overcome your demons, your insecurities. I have learned to embrace those vulnerabilities. It is of the utmost importance as an artist, to possess a healthy ego, which very much includes insecurity. Otherwise, you are merely someone who is a show-off and I have never admired that kind of performer.

So there seems to be an uneasiness that continues to live within me. Perhaps that is not altogether a bad thing. Perhaps I need it. Perhaps it feeds my hunger to create and the 'scared young girl' part of me is the most wonderful part of me. It urges me to continue to create and to keep going, whatever.

Recently, I was going over some lyrics I wrote for the character Isabelle in my play *Woman's Best Friend* (music by Greg Crease). I had no idea while writing them that some of these lyrics, even though they are character driven, are in part autobiographical.

'Looking For The Light'
When I look back at the girl I used to be
A total stranger is staring back at me
A girl full of joy
She has the boy
There's no other girl she'd rather be
If I'm honest, I'd say
Can't remember the day
The day it all came crumbling down
The day the smile changed to a frown
The day the light began to fade in me
Now my secret's out
What's my life about?
Is she there, the girl I used to be?

I'm looking for the light again
Looking for that girl again
Can't remember how to start
Mine is not an open heart
Guess I'll play my part again

I'm searching for a way to be
To try to come to terms with me
Can't remember how to dance
That's all caught up with romance
That's a thing my eyes don't see

There's no escaping it
I've been a fool
Thinking I could alter every rule
Hoping I could play the game
Wishing things would stay the same
Trying to hold on and stay cool
There's no escaping it
I've wasted time
Holding on to anger is a crime
How to let it go?
How to really know
That the girl I want to be is in her prime

I'm looking for the light to trace
Trusting there is nothing else to face
Open windows to embrace
Can I see things through with grace?
Looking for the light
Knowing it's in sight
Can I be the girl I used to be?

Although I have wished it, I have never felt a true connection to my immediate family. I have continued to blame myself for that. Surely it is my fault that we were never close? Could I have done more, felt more? It remains a constant, unanswered question in my life.

I love my brother, Leigh. We don't speak of the family at all really. Anyway, he doesn't remember much of any of it. He has been successful in blocking it out. Well, he has worked out his life in such a way that he chooses not to remember.

Like most people in show business, I have been searching for acceptance all my life, from audiences and colleagues. After all, family is who loves you.

My family is Brian and our beloved dogs, our divine, loving groodles, Pearl and Claude, and all those dogs that have left us, as well as any future babies. Our dogs' ashes are kept in our bedroom with us, sitting on my old oak chest of drawers, with their favourite toy alongside, guarding each of them.

My friends, like darling Les McDonald, who owns the iconic The Bookshop in Darlinghurst in Sydney have been totally supportive of me for as long as I can remember. He has been present at every decade birthday of mine since I turned thirty. My inner circle of friends, and they know who they are, have been there for me always. They know who I am and they love me for all my flaws, the way it is supposed to be with family. That'll do me. Yes. That'll do me.

It is still difficult to think of that young, frightened, though rebellious girl, being chastised constantly, being told every day that whatever she did she was not enough, being devastatingly embarrassed by her mother's behaviour, dreading the next night of domestic violence that she knew was just around the corner, waiting always for the next axe to fall and hoping against hope to avoid it. It was an achievement to live through it all, come out the other side and to go on to succeed in her much loved profession.

My mother was infuriating, sometimes frightening, and, yes, quite crazy.

And yet, she could be achingly funny, and extremely kind when you least expected it. I understand her more, now that I am older. I think I understand her unhappiness, the feeling that perhaps her best years were behind her, and her great sense of loss about a life she craved, but could never quite grasp.

I will never understand the outbursts on the bus and other places or exactly what triggered them. All I do know is there was a deep sadness in her, a sadness born out of trauma; a sadness no-one could reach, certainly not my father. I fear that, whatever had happened to her, it was much worse than what had happened to me when I was seventeen, after the *New Faces* win. And that is a devastating thought.

I wish, now that I am the age I am, that I could sit with her quietly and talk. Maybe we could connect, really connect. Maybe she could trust me enough to tell me what happened to her. Maybe now, with my life experience, I would know exactly what to say to get her to open up. I wouldn't push the wrong buttons in her and end up in a screaming match. And I could see her mouth twist ever so slightly, so that you never knew if she was about to yell at you or laugh. And when she did surprise you and laugh, her face would become young and playful, like a naughty schoolgirl holding on to a secret. I'd love to see that again, Izzie in full flight, looking youthful, riddled with childlike glee.

I have been thinking about what I know about life, what I have learned along the way. My conclusion is I have learnt a great deal, and yet I still don't know much. Above all else that I know about my life, I do know this: I love my mother.

Years ago when I was seeing that counsellor, we discussed that I have always been trying to be who I think men want me to be, trying to please and placate and smooth over things. Exhausting myself by trying to show them what a good person I am. Opening myself up too much, not setting boundaries, for the fear of losing them, so that they can't help but walk all over me. After all, it is human nature to do that. Observe the chink. Come in for the kill. My mother always used that well, knowing she could win by unnerving me and smashing through my defensive shell at her will.

I discovered through therapy that at other times I am a closed book. I simply shut down so nobody can get to me. I often shut down and don't get back to people when I should, simply because I don't have the capacity to do so. Life has become too much for me on that particular day.

My psychologist sets up an analogy: 'Think of yourself as a house. A healthy house is welcoming, but the front door is closed. Perhaps the windows are ajar or partially open to let the breeze in. There is a hearty fire crackling in the living room, off the kitchen. There is a welcoming ambience. All of the doors and windows are not flung wide open for all to see everything inside. Neither are they all slammed shut and locked so that nobody can get in.'

I think about that a lot.

I will be that house.

NEW YORK POST
'How to sing Sondheim ... you don't have to find a way to do it. You just do it. Other singers should see Geraldine Turner for that understanding alone.'

DAS WELT
'An earthquake hits Berlin.'

THE SYDNEY MORNING HERALD
'A legend this side of heaven.'

THE AGE
'A star worth selling the family silver to see.'

THE AUSTRALIAN
'A confident, commanding and astonishingly versatile talent.'

THE SONDHEIM REVIEW
'Miss Turner presented a Desirée who is not afraid to be direct. Her outstanding Desirée is a brilliantly beguiling and heartfelt performance.'

SHOW MUSIC
'Geraldine Turner's Reno Sweeney is brassy, loud and raucous in the best Merman tradition; she takes hold of the part and effortlessly walks away with the show. She proves again she has the best legit voice in the country.'

MUSICAL THEATRE ON RECORD
'Australia's Reno Sweeney ... and the role might have been written for her. She has not only a strong, vibrant chest voice, even and pleasant throughout its whole considerable range, but she has the evident ability as an actress and, above all, as a comedienne. Laughter twinkles through even her lustiest tones ... one, big sizzling joy.'